Y0-BPU-602

PUBLICATION NUMBER 10

Duke University Commonwealth-Studies Center

The Commonwealth Economy
in Southeast Asia

Duke University Commonwealth-Studies Center Publications

1. *The British Commonwealth: An Experiment in Co-operation among Nations,* by Frank H. Underhill

2. *South Africa: Economic and Political Aspects,* by Hector Menteith Robertson

3. *Some Comparative Aspects of Irish Law,* by Alfred Gaston Donaldson

4. *Economic Analysis and Policy in Underdeveloped Countries,* by P. T. Bauer

5. *The Higher Public Service of the Commonwealth of Australia,* by Howard A. Scarrow

6. *Economic Opinion and Policy in Ceylon,* by Henry M. Oliver, Jr.

7. *Problems of the New Commonwealth,* by Sir Ivor Jennings

8. *Commonwealth Perspectives,* by Nicholas Mansergh *et al.*

9. *Evolving Canadian Federalism,* by A. R. M. Lower, F. R. Scott, *et al.*

10. *The Commonwealth Economy in Southeast Asia,* by T. H. Silcock

The Commonwealth Economy
in Southeast Asia

T. H. Silcock

Professor of Economics
University of Malaya

PUBLISHED FOR THE

Duke University Commonwealth-Studies Center

DUKE UNIVERSITY PRESS, DURHAM, N. C.

CAMBRIDGE UNIVERSITY PRESS, LONDON

1959

© 1959, Duke University Press

Cambridge University Press, London, N. W. 1, England

The Library of Congress has cataloged this publication as follows:

Silcock, T H

 The Commonwealth economy in Southeast Asia. Durham, N. C., Published for the Duke University Commonwealth-Studies Center ₍by₎ Duke University Press, 1959.

 xix, 259 p. 21 cm. (Duke University Commonwealth-Studies Center. Publication no. 10)

 Bibliography : p. 216–250.

 1. Gt. Brit.—Colonies—Asia, Southeastern—Econ. condit. 2. Asia, Southeastern—Econ. condit. I. Title. (Series: Duke University, Durham, N. C. Commonwealth-Studies Center. Publications, no. 10)

HC412.S58   330.959   59–7085

Library of Congress

LIBRARY
FLORIDA STATE UNIVERSITY
TALLAHASSEE, FLORIDA

PRINTED IN THE UNITED STATES OF AMERICA

BY THE SEEMAN PRINTERY, INC., DURHAM, N. C.

TO H. T. SILCOCK

FOREWORD

SINCE the war the term "underdeveloped country"—
John Stuart Mill used the expression "backward country"
—has come into widespread use. In fact, the connota-
tive function of this term has almost superseded its
denotative function. The countries of the world have,
in effect, been distributed between two quite vaguely
defined classes, the developed and the underdeveloped,
the members of either of which may have little more in
common with one another than possession of an attribute
or two. Thus, as a rule, countries in which per capita
incomes are relatively high are described as developed;
countries in which they are low are labeled underdeveloped. Such a system of classification, though not without value, is too primitive and hence too arbitrary to
contribute greatly to analysis. Moreover, it blankets out
the great heterogeneity of both the relatively more and
the relatively less developed parts of the world. It passes
over all too lightly such facts as that in some so-called
underdeveloped countries average income may be five or
six times as high as in others, or that in some of these
countries the rate of natural increase may be two or
three times what it is in others. It is coming to be
recognized, therefore, that use must be made of numerous

classificatory criteria so that the heterogeneity of the "underdeveloped" (as of the "developed") world may be taken adequately into account, descriptively and analytically.

A very real contribution to the business of making students as well as publicists aware of the heterogeneity of the so-called underdeveloped world is made by Professor T. H. Silcock in the present study, one of a number being brought out under the auspices of the Duke University Commonwealth-Studies Center and treating of economic and political problems of countries with earmarks of underdevelopment. Not only does Professor Silcock deal with a very distinct part of Asia—Malaya, Singapore, Sarawak, Brunei and North Borneo—; he also demonstrates that each of these countries, two (i.e., Singapore, Malaya) situated on or at the extremity of the mainland and the others located in the northern portion of Borneo some five hundred miles from Malaya, differs from the others.

The diversity of these lands is reflected, for example, in their population density, ranging from that of Singapore, which is nearly comparable in density with Hong Kong, to that of Sarawak and North Borneo, which resembles the Belgian Congo in sparseness of population. It is reflected as well in differences in average income, which, while higher in Singapore than elsewhere in Asia (exclusive of Israel), is quite low in Sarawak and Borneo, though superior to that found in many parts of Asia. These lands resemble one another in that each rests upon an economic base which, though somewhat unique, is relatively narrow and not greatly variegated. In his first chapter Professor Silcock describes in considerable detail the characteristics of each of the Commonwealth lands under analysis, highlighting similarities and dissimi-

larities and indicating their significance for the future
course of economic development in this region.

Each of the countries is confronted by a somewhat
unique developmental problem. There is, of course, a
need everywhere for capital, in Singapore to offset a very
high rate of population growth and to undergird trade
more strongly with industry, in the Federation to get
more industry started and generally to give support to the
newly established Federation's protectionism, and elsewhere to facilitate the exploitation of natural wealth.
There is need everywhere, especially outside Singapore, for
skilled personnel, just as there is need for the maintenance
of suitable external marketing connections. There is
everywhere a population problem, with Singapore overcrowded and with Malaya likely to become overcrowded
in the future, but with the Borneo lands still short of
enough people to carry through their development most
effectively. Nonetheless, despite these similarities, the
inhabitants of each land are confronted by a particular
set of concrete developmental problems, since each land
possesses a somewhat unique collection of resources, exploitation of which is handicapped also in several instances
by ethnic and cultural diversity and political strife. These
problems and the circumstances giving rise to them are
carefully and judiciously treated by Professor Silcock,
together with divers means available for surmounting
these problems, particularly in his third and fifth chapters.

The countries under discussion are as advanced as
they are because, through the medium of a now somewhat
irrationally condemned relationship—that which con-
nected Britain and her colonies—superior techniques and
capital and personnel flowed into these lands from abroad
and raised the level of their economic performance above
that found in neighboring countries. The old relation-

ship has now been replaced in varying measure by that realized, or eventually to be realized, within the framework of the Commonwealth and the sterling area—a relationship that emphasized local autonomy, co-operation, and complementarities. The new relationship is discussed by Professor Silcock in his second chapter, in which he examines "the Commonwealth impact" and contrasts this impact with that experienced under an earlier colonial or protected status. He also points (late in his third chapter) to the educational, scholarly, technical, commercial, and related contributions which the United States can make to the development of these lands and to the accentuation of a beneficial Commonwealth impact. The significance of Europe's expanding free trade area for the development of Malaya and Singapore is dealt with in the fourth chapter.

In a most interesting final chapter Professor Silcock isolates the determinants of economic development which seem to be of most relevance to the areas about which he is writing. He examines these in the socioeconomic context of the areas and shows, for example, that while there is great need for business education, this education needs to be accommodated to the forms of business organization in use among the Chinese, Indians, and others. He delineates the role which government may play in fostering economic development in Southeast Asia. And so on.

The reader of this volume is bound to have his appetite whetted for more about the interesting parts of the world treated therein. He will find, at the close of the last chapter, a fairly long list of books and articles, subdivided into nineteen categories and sufficiently annotated to indicate the nature and the quality of the contents of the pieces listed.

This judicious, carefully written, and forward looking volume reflects in its conception and in its rich and thoughtful detail the close acquaintance of its author with the countries discussed and with their problems. It reflects his extensive knowledge of the economies of Southeast Asia and his experience in the conduct of surveys (e.g., of Sarawak), and with the Economic Commission for Asia and the Far East. It manifests his concern with the implications of economic theory for the discovery of workable developmental policies. It reflects finally his many years of experience, in a varied professional association with the University of Malaya as professor of economics and university administrator, with the educational problems of Southeast Asia, and with the potentially great role that education can play in the unfolding of this region's economic potential.

Since the Commonwealth-Studies Center is concerned exclusively with the encouragement of research, specific theories or interpretations of Commonwealth affairs appearing in these publications do not constitute an expression of the view of the Center or of the Carnegie Corporation, which has furnished financial support to the Center. The respective authors of the several publications are responsible for the conclusions expressed in them.

JOSEPH J. SPENGLER

INTRODUCTORY STATEMENT

I AM GRATEFUL to Duke University for the opportunity first of giving these lectures in the United States and now of presenting them to the public. At the time I was first invited to give them, Malaya was still a protected Federal State, but by the time they were delivered it had become an independent member of the Commonwealth. While they were in press the first full-scale international conference, a meeting of the United Nations Economic Commission for Asia and the Far East, was held on independent Malayan soil. It seemed appropriate that the lectures should deal with Malaya's growth to independent status.

As an economist, I had to deal primarily with the economic aspects of this development; and this implied dealing with the economy of Malaya as a whole, a united economy undergoing marked changes as a result of this political transformation.

It soon became clear that even Malaya was too narrow. The economy of Singapore has many external links, but the links with the three territories in northern Borneo include a common currency and common political institutions. Moreover, in some respects these territories are closely similar to Malaya at an earlier stage of political and economic development.

For these reasons I decided to attempt to deal with the economy of all the Commonwealth territories in the region. The emphasis, however, was uneven. Neither North Borneo nor Hong Kong could be omitted in surveying the general pattern, though my personal knowledge of these territories is slight. I have included them within the over-all survey of the region, but the analysis and examples are drawn mainly from Malaya, Singapore, and Sarawak.

Yet in dealing with the region's economy I have not found it practicable to treat it merely as a case study in the increasingly fashionable subject of economic growth. The timing of the lectures virtually compelled me to deal with Malaya's rapid progress to self-government. It might have seemed appropriate to draw a parallel between economic and political growth: to show an economic structure supporting and drawing strength from a political structure, and both developing in harmony. The facts, however, do not support such an approach.

The process of political development appears to foster institutions and relations in the economic sphere which become inappropriate, once the controlling power is no longer there. A discontinuity in economic growth seems likely, a discontinuity which is closely related to the process of political development that prevails in all the countries with non-European populations in the Commonwealth.

Such a discontinuity is not necessarily harmful. The fact that independence involves substantial changes in economic structure may stimulate new attitudes and relationships that will provide new momentum. But this is sufficiently unlikely to make it worthwhile to examine in some detail why the discontinuity occurs.

For the discontinuity is not simply a breaking of ancient chains, as a simple nationalist might suppose. It differs from this almost as much as it differs from the optimistic picture of an orderly method of political growth, tried out over centuries among nations with English (or at least European) peoples, and now miraculously proving its efficacy even for nations less fortunately endowed.

There are real difficulties in transferring to countries where the Europeans are the entrepreneurs and civil servants a pattern of political development which worked well enough when they were the whole population. I have attempted to analyze these, for the area of Southeast Asia with which I am familiar, in these lectures to an American audience, not only because I hope this may improve American understanding of the non-European parts of the Commonwealth, but because I believe it may stimulate American acts and attitudes that will help the Commonwealth to solve its own problems.

I have retained the informal style used in delivering the lectures, but have included some extra material. I have also added as Chapter IV a short paper on Malaya and the European Free Trade Area, which amplifies a point in Chapter III. Permission to publish this in the United States simultaneously with its publication in England as part of a study of the Commonwealth and the European Free Trade Area has been generously given by the United Kingdom Council of the European Movement, the publishers of the latter study.

Chapter V is a short essay on economic development of countries of the type found in Southeast Asia. Although based on a lecture given at the International Economic Association's postgraduate course in Singapore in 1956, it has been substantially rewritten for the *Malayan Economic Review* and is, therefore, like Chapter IV, rather less informal than the first three chapters. My thanks are due to the editor of the *Malayan Economic Review* for permission to reproduce it here.

Inevitably, anyone who works in a region which is not well documented is more than usually indebted for information and stimulus to personal contacts, and it is a pleasure to record some of my debts here. For increased understanding of the general pattern of Southeast Asian economics I am indebted to fellow consultants and colleagues at the United Nations Economic Commission for Asia and the Far East, especially Mr. U Tun Wai now of the International Monetary Fund, Professor Shigeto Tsuru of Hitotsubashi University and Mr. T. Y. Wu of the ECAFE

Secretariat. My former Vice Chancellor, Sir Sydney Caine, and my colleagues in the University of Malaya, especially Dean Lim Tay Boh and Ungku Abdul Aziz, have informed and corrected me, and I have learned from the questions and presuppositions of my students. I have drawn on the deep knowledge concerning the economies of Malaya and Singapore of Dr. F. C. C. Benham, Mr. O. A. Spencer, and Mr. B. A. St. J. Hepburn. Some of these economists and government officers would dissent, perhaps sharply, from some of my analysis; and they cannot, of course, be held responsible for my errors.

Finally, I wish to express my thanks to Miss Margaret Flinter for generous and skilful help in the typing and preparation of the manuscript.

T. H. SILCOCK

University of Malaya
Singapore
May, 1958

CONTENTS

The Commonwealth Economy
in Southeast Asia

The Basic Pattern

THE COMMONWEALTH ECONOMY in Southeast Asia must be seen in relation to Southeast Asia as a whole, a region not without importance in the modern world because it is a region of potential instability and of potential prosperity. It is a region of comparatively small countries, mostly with new and not very strong governments, and it is rather overshadowed by the great masses of India and of China, both of which have substantial minority populations scattered through the region. Most of the economies of these countries follow the colonial pattern of specialization on a comparatively small number of primary export products. This specialization made them in the past highly dependent on trade with the more developed countries of the West. The United States, for example, still relies heavily on the region for rubber and tin and a number of other less important products.

Formerly, this trade was secured by the control over most of the countries of the region exercised by

the Western powers: the French in the area known
as Indo-China, the Dutch in Indonesia, the Americans in the Philippines, and the British in most of the
rest of the region. Before the Second World War
only Thailand in the whole area had retained its
independence, and Thailand's dependence on international trade was only indirectly safeguarded by
colonial rule, which safeguarded the trade of the
region and hence insured the surplus which enabled
several of the countries to buy Thailand's rice.

I am not here to defend this colonial structure
which brought the countries of the region considerable instability along with a higher standard of living, taking good years with bad, than the rest of
Asia. It was in any event inevitably a temporary
phase, though the colonial powers (with the exception
of the United States) were not particularly conscious
of this. I am concerned rather to discuss the current
needs of the region arising out of this colonial phase
and particularly out of its disintegration. But the
parts of the region with which I am particularly
concerned are those within the Commonwealth of
Nations, whether as colonies in the last stages of
colonialism or as independent countries.

Apart from their specialization, there are some
other basic features which most of the Southeast
Asian countries have in common. All of them have
rates of population growth which are high by the
standards of the rest of the world, some of them very
high indeed; for example, Singapore's rate of approximately 3½ per cent per annum and the equal or

higher rate in Taiwan. For the most part, however, these countries are not overpopulated, since they all lie within a region where public health services introduced by the colonial powers have made an enormous difference in the populations which can be supported. Except for the island of Java, virtually the whole area of the Malay Peninsula and the vast range of islands in its neighborhood remained almost completely empty until about a century ago, in spite of the close proximity of the overcrowded areas of India and China. The terrain was difficult, unhealthy, and unattractive.

A good deal of land is therefore still available for development in Burma, Thailand, Malaya, and the outer islands of Indonesia. The main difficulties of developing it are not really economic. Such economic difficulties as there are, are closely related to the acceleration in the rate of population growth.[1] Phenomena of land hunger, such as high rents and large numbers of landless peasants, have emerged in several countries where it was formerly possible for the population to spread into new uninhabited areas as it slowly increased in numbers. This seems to be due partly to the fact that population increase is more rapid, partly to the complexity of administration which makes the settlement of new land a more complicated task, and partly to much higher standards of social and economic services which have made it more of an adventure to move out of settled areas

[1] Marshall C. Balfour, et al., Public Health and Demography in the Far East (New York: Rockefeller Foundation, 1950).

into uninhabited ones. Scarcities of administrative talent and economic enterprise are being felt, and the capital cost of new land development is likely to strain the capacity to save of many of these countries. There are empty lands, but with a rapidly increasing population, there is a scarcity of the complementary factors of enterprise, administration, and capital which would enable them to be filled.

Another feature common to much of the Southeast Asian economy is the presence of specialist migrant groups which have performed essential functions in economic development but have not been assimilated into the population. The most important of these groups is the overseas Chinese, but there are also overseas Indians and some migrants between the Southeast Asian territories.

In this complex and important economic region, it is our present task to investigate the impact on economic development of some of the features of British colonial administration and of the pattern of development from colonial status to independence within the Commonwealth. We shall, therefore, be concerned mainly with the following political units and the economies which support them. First, we have the Federation of Malaya, which has recently achieved the status of independence within the Commonwealth. Included in the Federation of Malaya but differing from it in some of its political and economic aspects is the free port of Penang. Next, we have the other great entrepôt ports of Singapore and Hong Kong, of which the former has recently acquired complete internal self-government, while the latter occupies a special and unique position in relation to the sterling area because of its situation as an entrepôt for mainland China.[2] Next there are the two colonial territories of North Borneo and Sarawak, and between them the small but exceptionally prosperous protected state of Brunei. Incorporated within North Borneo but differing from it in some of its economic characteristics is the island of Labuan, a former settlement of the Colony of the Straits Settlements, while on the opposite side of North Borneo the small port of Tawau shows sign of developing into another entrepôt port.

These are the territories in the Southeast Asian area which lie within the Commonwealth, though we shall have occasion also to refer to three other Commonwealth features within the region and to some of its relations with the Commonwealth countries of India, Ceylon, and Australia on its outskirts.

The three additional features are, first, the role of the office of the Commissioner General for Southeast Asia in the economy and its development during the twelve years since the war; next, the Colombo Plan, which began as a Commonwealth venture and has now extended its influence over the economies of most of Southeast Asia; and finally the position of the Union of Burma, which took the unusual step of emerging from colonial status to complete independence of the Commonwealth while retaining its mem-

[2] Special Correspondent, "Monetary Systems of the Colonies," *The Banker*, LXXXVII (Oct., 1948), 21-24.

bership in the sterling area, and so remaining partly within the Commonwealth economic system.

In the remainder of this chapter I shall give a brief account of the economic structure of the countries to which I have referred and in subsequent chapters shall try to assess some of the impacts of British colonial techniques and the pattern of development towards independent status within the Commonwealth on the economic problems of these territories.

The Federation of Malaya is normally regarded as an economy dependent on the export of rubber and tin. This is substantially a correct picture but perhaps conveys inadequately the predominance of rubber, and also the importance of the entrepôt trade to Malaya's prosperity. Tin has had a very great impact on the public finance of Malaya, and by making it possible to build roads and railways out of current income and to develop a fairly elaborate structure of government it has been partly responsible for the growth of the rubber industry. But at least ten people are employed directly or indirectly by the rubber industry for every one employed directly or indirectly by the tin industry. And the impact of fluctuations in the price of rubber on Malaya's national income is far greater than that of fluctuations in the price of tin. Natural latex is Malaya's life blood; and by engaging a substantial proportion of its development appropriations in replanting programs, Malaya has invested heavily in the future competitive capacity of natural rubber in rivalry with synthetic.

Like most countries which have colonial economies (i.e., economies heavily dependent on a narrow range of primary export products[3]) Malaya as it achieves independence is attempting to secure greater diversification and some industrialization. Some of its most important problems, however, are problems of the rubber industry. For example, economic trends appear to indicate that the estate form of production may secure greater relative advantages in the future than it has enjoyed in the past, since the yield per acre of modern high-yielding trees cannot be increased greatly (if at all) by the close-planting techniques which have given smallholders in the past a rather higher yield per acre from unselected rubber than estates.[4] Moreover, the trend toward export of latex and of technically classified rubber at present favors the estates, though it may be possible to develop suitable techniques for smallholders to follow this trend. Political trends on the other hand clearly favor the relative expansion of the smallholdings by encouraging new planting of rubber by smallholders. Supplies of external capital are less likely to be forthcoming than in the past, and the estate form of organization is widely believed in the industry to be incapable of operation on the present

[3] B. K. Madan, ed., *Economic Problems of Underdeveloped Countries in Asia* (London: Oxford University Press, 1954).

[4] P. T. Bauer, *Report on a Visit to Rubber Growing Smallholdings in Malaya, July-September 1946* (Colonial Research Publication No. 1) (London: H. M. S. O., 1948).

scale, except by European personnel, which will clearly become less appropriate as political developments go forward.

If the judgment of the Malayan government concerning the future of natural rubber proves to be sound, Malaya will within a comparatively short period have returned to the position in the natural rubber market which it enjoyed before the ill-fated Stevenson Restriction Scheme stimulated massive new planting by smallholders in Sumatra in the 1920's. For Malaya, of all the major producing countries, has introduced the most far-reaching replanting scheme, financed by a levy on the export of rubber[5] and designed to replace most of its existing rubber trees by modern strains yielding about three times as much per acre.

In this scheme also there are problems arising from differences between different types of producers. We may distinguish four different categories, though the boundaries between them are by no means clear. There are efficient estates which, when the scheme was introduced, had already adopted a cycle of replanting designed to replace their stands of old rubber by new high-yielding varieties.[6] There are other estates which had done little or no replanting since the war and appeared to be operating their holdings as wasting assets. There are smallholdings of between ten and one hundred acres where labor is

[5] Federation of Malaya, *Taxation and Replanting in the Rubber Industry* (Kuala Lumpur: Government Printer, 1955).
[6] *Ibid.*, pp. 12-17, 37.

employed both in good times and in bad and where the owners are mainly non-Malays; and there are tiny peasant holdings, mainly Malay-owned, where labor may be employed when the price of rubber is high but where paid labor will normally be dispensed with, and the work done only by the family, when times are hard.[7]

Broadly speaking, we may say that the replanting scheme favors the second and third categories at the expense of the first and fourth, notwithstanding the fact that on economic grounds the first category (the efficient estates) should be favored and on political grounds the fourth (the Malay peasants) because of the universally admitted need to raise the economic status of the Malays and so make possible a balanced and united nation.

The small estates are compelled by financial pressures to replant and in effect are subsidized by the large estates which have already replanted, and hence have a higher yield and a higher payment of levy per acre, while drawing only the same benefit. The peasant smallholders are penalized because it is technically almost impossible to replant less than one acre and hence to introduce a reasonable replanting cycle on a plot of less than five acres, bearing in mind that rubber takes seven years to produce any revenue. The grant from the replanting scheme approximately covers a smallholder's cost of replanting but certainly

[7] Bauer, *Report on a Visit*; T. H. Silcock, "A Note on the Working of Rubber Regulation," *Economic Journal*, LVIII (June, 1948), 228-235.

does not compensate him for all the loss of income that he suffers by replanting, and this loss (even if it were proportional in smallholdings of all sizes) would be much harder for a peasant to bear.

I do not mean to suggest by this analysis that the replanting scheme is merely perverse. It can be argued that replanting can look after itself on the larger estates and that it is the smaller and less efficient which need a stimulus to replant. My own view is that these estates should have been allowed to sink or swim, and those which sank could have been bought up by the government and replanted with high-yielding material in model smallholdings for re-settlement (as suggested by Bauer). But this is perhaps a radical suggestion and would have been difficult to push through during the period of British control in face of the combined political and economic power of the rubber industry. As for the smallest smallholdings, it seems clear that planting of high-yielding strains is possible to them only if planting of new areas is allowed,[8] and to have allowed new planting initially would have made any enforcement of replanting at any level very difficult. The larger smallholdings, and even the estates, would have wanted new land for planting the high-yielding strains.

It can be said that in levying some U. S. $90 million for replanting in its five-year plan, the government is taking a more optimistic view of future

[8] P. T. Bauer, "Malayan Rubber Policy," *Political Science Quarterly*, LXXII (March, 1957), 83-99.

prospects for natural rubber than professional opera-
tors in the stock market. Probably, however, the
value of natural rubber shares is influenced at least
as much by political as by economic factors, and so far
as this is true, it is plainly in Malaya's interest to
check a long-run flight of capital by measures designed
to push reinvestment beyond what would be dictated
by natural economic forces. It seems probable that
some new planting, particularly by smallholders,
may also be encouraged, though it might be dangerous to expand acreage under natural rubber too
far.[9]

The chief problem confronting Malaya's tin industry is the rapid exhaustion of known tin-bearing
deposits. Prospecting has been delayed mainly by
Communist terrorism but also by the comparative
weakness of the state administrations which control
land policy and by some hostility among the Malays
toward expanding the area of tin mining. Further
factors often mentioned are the imposition of income
tax on a regular basis since the war and the fact that
general inflation has increased the burden of the
export duty on tin, the percentage of which rises as
tin prices rise.

Insofar as this last factor is operative, Malaya
seems to be paying the penalty for taking the government share of the tin exported from the country not
in a royalty negotiated separately for each area of

[9] Bauer rightly stresses that the effect on the price should not
be a major consideration. The danger rises from excessive
specialization of Malaya's economy.

land, but by an export duty, varying with the price but uniform for all producers. The export duty has enabled Malaya to derive part of the equity from inflation since the time of the discovery of the mines, but only at the cost of a proportionately heavier burden on new prospecting.

If new capital from outside Malaya is likely to be forthcoming, the simplest solution for this problem might be to convert all export duties into royalties payable to the state for existing properties by negotiation subject to compulsory arbitration, and to fix royalties on land discovered by new prospecting in accordance with current costs of development.[10]

If, on the other hand, new capital is not likely to be forthcoming, a simpler plan would be nationalization of tin mining, subject to a fair level of compensation such as would not frighten capital out of other industries. Any such nationalization, however, might threaten confidence in Malaya's industry generally, so that the more complex alternative would probably be a safer solution.

Malaya is also trying to promote the growth of a variety of minor industries, to improve its self-sufficiency in food, and to develop new export crops. The main problem in industrialization, which concerns the relations between the Federation

[10] The new constitution is concerned to give the states an interest in encouraging tin mining, but appears to envisage a continuation of export duty. Cf. Federation of Malaya, *Constitutional Proposals for the Federation of Malaya* (Kuala Lumpur: Government Printer, 1957), par. 39, p. 15; clause 110 (3), p. 77.

and Singapore, will be considered later. The problem of improving Malaya's food production is mainly one of increasing the output of rice. Increased production of rice has been handicapped mainly by the superior income-earning possibilities of rubber at all times between the two World Wars.[11] Whether in boom or in depression, rubber was the more profitable crop; and it would hardly be too much to say that almost all the rice produced in Malaya at this time was produced because of the unwillingness or inability of Malay farmers to desert their traditional pattern of agriculture for a more profitable system. The greater part of government policy was directed to checking the flow of Malays away from their traditional subsistence agriculture. We must be careful, however, not to overstate the case here, since a great deal of constructive work by the Department of Agriculture during the 1930's was just beginning to bear fruit when it was dissipated by the war and the Japanese occupation.

Greater production of rice in Malaya can occur on any substantial scale only if rubber falls drastically in price or if the income which can be obtained from rice growing increases. Some progress has been made since the war both in improving the strains of rice and in introducing mechanization. The average area of rice farms is, however, far too small; and one might almost say that if new land is not to be de-

[11] The *Report of the Rice Production Committee* (1953) gives too little attention to the inverse relation between rubber prices and rice output; but cf. *Final Report of the Rice Committee* (1957).

veloped by government initiative, the best thing that could happen to rice growing would be for very large numbers of peasants to leave the land permanently so as to increase the profitability of rice growing for those who remain. A better alternative would, of course, be the opening up of sufficient new areas for rice growing to absorb the new growth of population and some two-thirds of the existing peasants, so as to give each farmer a holding of a dozen acres or so.[12]

The soil of Malaya is not particularly suited to rice growing, and the climate makes irrigation necessary for large yields. While the traditional methods of Malay settlement were sufficient to make it possible for new holdings of three to five acres[13] to be developed, to keep pace with the slower rate of population growth that seems to have prevailed until malaria was brought under control, the opening up of enough farms of economic size to cope with all those who could work them in modern conditions seems to be a task beyond the financial and administrative resources of existing state governments. Fragmentation of holdings, excessive rents, and land hunger do not in Malaya correspond to an excess of population over existing cultivable land but rather to a rise in the level of living expected (because of the

[12] U. A. Aziz, "Facts and Fallacies of Malay Economy," *Straits Times,* Singapore. A series of four articles, February 28 to March 5, 1957.

[13] See E. H. G. Dobby, "The Kelantan Delta," *Geographical Review,* XLI (April, 1951), 226-255, for traditional methods of settlement.

development of rubber) and a rise in the rate of population growth without any corresponding increase in the rate of development of new land.

Much is made in government reports of the exploitation of peasants by traders and landlords. It appears to be true that the cultural background of the trading community (which is mainly Chinese) has developed greater financial sophistication among them than among rural Malays, and that peasants tend to lose their land and to get heavily into debt. It is hardly helpful, however, to attribute this situation to the extortionate ways of the traders or alternatively to the improvidence of the peasants. There may well be abnormal social conditions which weaken the power of Malay peasants to resist the combination of the normal farmer's shortage of short-term capital and the availability of credit on onerous terms. Similarly, there may be special social forces which inhibit competition among Chinese traders. If so, it will be necessary to deal with these problems by research[14] followed by extension work. But it is necessary to look also at the underlying economic forces, namely, the impact on a subsistence economy of higher standards of living elsewhere, an increasing rate of growth of population, and a failure of land settlement to proceed sufficiently fast to counter these pressures.

To get more rice per head it will be necessary for

[14] I have been privileged to see a Report on Field-Work in Batu Pahat, at present unpublished, by Dr. K. O. L. Burridge, which (in part) deals with these problems.

the cultivators to farm more land per head. This
is mainly a problem of opening up more land by
road-building, irrigation, etc. The difficulties are
mainly administrative and political and will be discussed in the next chapter. Insofar as they are economic difficulties, they are part of the general Southeast Asian pattern of rising social standards in the
inhabited areas inflating the capital cost of developing new land. Indonesia's experience in trying to
persuade population to move from the highly developed but overcrowded island of Java to the undeveloped parts of the outer islands shows this difficulty
most clearly. Malaya's development has been concentrated in the capitals, the trading ports, and the
estates and mines, so that it is not so difficult for
Malaya to afford to match, in new areas, the standards
of existing peasant areas.

We turn next to a sketch of the economies of the
three British territories in Borneo.

Perhaps the most important point to be made
about these three territories is that, although they are
all in many ways very underdeveloped, they are surprisingly different from one another.

The comparatively backward economic develop-
ment of Sarawak is not due to being recently sub-
jected to Western influence. Part of Sarawak has
been a British dependency longer than any of the
Malay States which now make up the Federation of
Malaya. Resources may be inferior to those of the
Malay Peninsula, although they are not markedly so.
The comparatively backward level of development

is the result of deliberate policy of the Brooke family, who were hereditary rajahs and who were averse to allowing extensive development by European capital or education of the indigenous races. Their object appears to have been first to suppress head-hunting and thereafter to encourage gradual development of commercial crops by local enterprise and to govern through a small educated elite of Malays.

Since the cession of Sarawak to the British Crown by the last rajah in 1947, the policy of development has changed in many ways. Education among the indigenous races has been expanded, even though the expansion was very gradual;[15] a series of development plans has been initiated and carried through, so far as shortages of staff and building labor permitted;[16] and political development through local government authorities has made some progress.[17]

The basic demographic structure of Sarawak is that it is extremely sparsely populated with barely one-tenth of the population of the Federation of Malaya in an area almost as large.[18] This population is divided into three racial groups: the pagan peoples,

[15] E. W. Woodhead, *Report upon Financing of Education and Conditions of Service in the Teaching Profession in Sarawak* (Kuching: Government Printer, 1955).

[16] "Memorandum on Development in Sarawak, 1947" (mimeographed: Sarawak Government); *Development Plan of Sarawak, 1955-60* (Kuching: Government Printer, 1954); *Reports on Development, 1952-1955* (Kuching: Government Printer).

[17] Sarawak, *Annual Reports on Sarawak, 1948-1956* (Kuching: Government Printer).

[18] J. L. Noakes, *A Report on the 1947 Population Census of Sarawak* (London: Crown Agents for the Colonies, 1950).

of whom the Iban or Sea Dyaks are much the strongest both numerically and in individual vigor; next, the Malays, who were until the cession the administrative and intellectual elite but are now being replaced in this position by the wealthier and probably better educated Chinese. The third group is this large and rapidly increasing Chinese population which controls nearly all the business and a substantial part of the pepper and timber industries.

Economically, Sarawak's economy depends on four products: rubber, pepper, oil, and timber.[19] The relative importance of these products is a matter of definition, but on almost any showing rubber will rank as most important. In certain years exports of rubber have been exceeded by those of pepper, but rubber employs far more people, being much more of a smallholder's crop, while a fairly high proportion of the pepper gardens are owned by comparatively wealthy Chinese in the mixed zones (or areas where land can be held by all races) along the few roads and some of the principal rivers. Oil might be regarded as much the most important product in Sarawak if we judge by the export figures alone. This is the result of the fact that the first oil was struck in the north of Sarawak in the Miri area, while much larger reserves have since been found in Brunei. The result is that the refinery built at Lutong in Sarawak to handle the Sarawak oil production now refines virtually all the Brunei oil. This is imported into

[19] T. H. Silcock, *Fiscal Survey of Sarawak* (Sarawak: Government Printer, 1956).

Sarawak by a pipe line and re-exported by another pipe line out to sea, through which the tankers are loaded some miles from the coast. Because of the great importance of the Brunei oil field, the largest in the Commonwealth, even the value added in the refinery constitutes an important part of Sarawak's national income, but its contribution to employment is very small. Finally, the timber industry is the one which has been developing most rapidly in recent years and appears to have the greatest potentiality of growth.

One of the most striking features of the Sarawak rubber industry is the responsiveness of the supply to price changes.[20] Estate rubber is normally produced in more or less constant quantities regardless of the price, except when a restriction scheme is imposed. Some rubber smallholders are equally unresponsive to price changes, though they may employ less labor for the same output at low prices. The smallholders of Sarawak and Sumatra, however, often grow rubber as part of a process of shifting cultivation, growing their crop of rice for one or two years on cleared jungle land and then planting rubber instead of allowing the natural growth of jungle. Such rubber will be tapped when it is worth tapping, but the person who planted it normally has alternative sources of income if the price of rubber is not sufficiently attractive to cover the trouble and transport cost.

The apparent fluctuation in the output of rubber is probably even greater than the real fluctuation

[20] *Ibid.*

because of rubber smuggled through Sarawak from South Borneo, which is part of Indonesia. At fairly high prices rubber grown on the Indonesian side of the frontier will bear the costs of transport up the river, portage over land, accommodation to Indonesian customs officials, and transport down to the Sarawak port of shipment, so earning foreign exchange for the export of capital or purchase of luxury goods. The Sarawak government, which derives export duty from this trade, does not inquire too closely into the origin of the rubber.

Even the genuine fluctuations in the output of rubber are considerable. This causes some instability in the Sarawak economy but contributes something to stabilizing the price of rubber in the world market. Probably the relative importance of smallholders has been a significant factor, along with the growth of the synthetic rubber industry, contributing to the rather greater stability of rubber since the Second World War. Before the war, except when it was covered by a restriction scheme, rubber was probably the most volatile in price of all important commodities in the world.[21]

Sarawak, like Malaya, has its own replanting scheme. There is keen awareness of the probable long-run decline in rubber prices and the need to increase productivity to compete with synthetic rubber. Replanting, however, is an extremely difficult problem because of the wide variety of conditions in which

[21] UNECAFE, *Economic Bulletin for Asia and the Far East*. Semi-Annual Survey, Aug., 1954.

rubber is grown, the great differences between Sarawak and Malaya, and the enormous difficulty of extension work for smallholders among so ignorant and scattered a population. There has been some useful co-operation with the Rubber Research Institute in Malaya, but although a good deal of interest has been shown by rubber smallholders in bud-grafting, the problem of replanting has as yet barely been tackled.

The pepper industry is one which has made a minor contribution to the Sarawak economy for many years, and Sarawak pepper is a special grade that enjoys some prestige in the world market. It was only in the late forties and early fifties, however, that pepper came to be for a short while Sarawak's leading crop.[22] The Japanese invasion had largely destroyed the pepper industry in Southeast Asia, and with the restoration of more normal ways of living pepper shot up to fabulous prices, and many acres of pepper gardens were opened up along the main rivers and roads of Sarawak. With the collapse of the pepper price, many of these gardens would in any event have been abandoned, but pepper disease has also attacked the country, and the industry has now fallen back to a relatively minor position in Sarawak's economy.

The oil industry is better discussed in relation to Brunei. Large parts of Sarawak have not yet been surveyed, and it is possible that further oil supplies

[22] Sarawak, *Annual Reports*, *1950-1956*; Silcock, *Fiscal Survey*.

will be discovered. The chief hope seems to be the discovery of further deposits of oil under the sea off the Sarawak coast.

The timber industry, which mainly depends on the cutting of a special Sarawak timber called ramin, is one in which the government is in a position to derive revenue from a situation of temporary monopoly. Ramin is not produced in quantity anywhere except in Sarawak, and no softwood of similar quality is obtainable except from dollar sources. Until 1955 production was increasing quite rapidly but without depressing the price. Eventually the expansion caused a fall in ramin prices as well as fears that there was overcutting by small producers.

We can best discuss the forestry problem in connection with North Borneo, where there has been more controversy about it. But if restriction of cutting is desired to exploit Sarawak's temporary monopoly, resulting from exchange restrictions on dollar competition, the best way to do this would probably be to raise the royalty rather than foster monopoly within the industry by a stricter licensing system and control of cutting.

One of the timber industry's chief contributions to the economy of Sarawak is that it provides casual employment for the young men of the pagan tribes, particularly the Iban. This experience of working with machinery and more or less modern capitalistic methods may in time have a radical influence on the economy of the inland long-houses to which these men return.

Three minor crops of Sarawak may be worth a brief mention. Sago production enjoyed a brief period of prosperity after the war, and this stimulated both overcutting of the sago gardens and mechanization of the rasping process.[23] The aftereffects on the economy of the rather primitive Melanau people who cultivate the sago have been very serious, and there seems some doubt whether the industry can recover unless there is another sharp rise in the world price of the product.

Jelutong, the raw material of chewing gum, is also collected in the jungles of Sarawak but has declined in importance with the development of supplies elsewhere.

The most interesting of the three is the illipe nut, from which an oil used in confectionery is derived. The trees grow wild but have also been planted on the banks of the rivers in the far interior. The harvest is irregular but occurs approximately every four years. Once in twenty years or so there will be a bumper crop such as that of 1954, when about two million dollars' worth of illipe nuts were exported. According to Iban land customs the ownership of these trees is often obscure,[24] and men may travel long distances to assert their right to the nuts planted by an ancestor.

Although primitive people, Iban are accus-

[23] H. S. Morris, *Report on a Melanau Sago Producing Community* (London: H. M. S. O., 1953).

[24] J. D. Freeman, *Iban Agriculture* (Colonial Research Studies, No. 18) (London: H. M. S. O., 1955); Sarawak, *Annual Report, 1954.*

tomed to trade, and before Cession the proceeds of a good harvest of illipe nuts would be invested in gongs and jars, which were the chief forms of durable wealth recognized by these people. Active salesmanship by private companies and some development efforts by government have persuaded many Iban to substitute outboard motors, which they use in their dug-out canoes, and also sewing machines and some rice mills as means of storing wealth. It is a matter of some interest for the traveler to find dried human heads hanging at one end of a long-house and to see a number of modern outboard motors stored at the other. It seems probable that if these people can be encouraged to abandon their long-houses and build individual dwellings, quite radical changes in capital formation may take place. It is often supposed that the practice of living with forty or more families housed within a single structure would make for a form of primitive communism. This appears to be a mistaken view of Iban culture, and the separate families are in fact much more aggressive individualists than the Malays, who live in separate houses.[25] They are essentially a frontier people, and the need to live in long-houses was a consequence first of the desire for protection against head-hunting and later a practice enforced by the administration as a means of indirect rule.

Both long-house life and shifting cultivation hamper capital formation because they set a pattern of living in which the accumulation of possessions is not

[25] Freeman, *Iban Agriculture*.

easy. But there are fewer mental barriers to radical economic changes than there are among other primitive peoples in the region.

The mention of outboard motors and the limitations imposed by long-house life brings us to the two most important features of Sarawak's economy: the need to develop transport and the backwardness of education. Like most of the island continent of Borneo, Sarawak lacks roads. The problem of developing more transport is indeed an exceptionally difficult one. The country is sparsely populated, and the natural means of transport are the great rivers along which all the settlements lie. Bars at the mouths of all the main rivers, except the Rejang, confine inland transport to small craft, while the rivers themselves and the heavy rainfall make road-building exceedingly expensive. Development by a road system has proceeded furthest in the extreme southwest, near Kuching, the capital. This area is largely isolated from the rest of the country. The great Rejang river system has an economy focused on Sibu in the third division, which it will take years of effort and millions of dollars to link to the road system around Kuching. Another road system is developing in the north of the country in the neighborhood of the oil fields, but the oil of Miri itself is running dry, and there seems little prospect of further extension of this system to link up with the rest of the economy unless more oil is discovered on land in Sarawak.

Under the present development plan the government is committed to a trunk-road system, which will reach into the interior from the first division,[26] and is also contemplating expenditure on improving the river system as a transport route. Scarcity of labor, however, at present makes the development of transport very costly.

At the time of the Cession, Sarawak confronted a far more difficult educational problem than even Malaya. Politically, the problem of creating a unified system for Chinese, Malays, and the pagan native peoples seemed almost insuperable. Malay education was centered in Islam and in the official system built up by the rajahs who had ruled through a Malay elite. There had been a good deal of missionary activity among the pagan peoples by rival Christian missions to whom the rajahs had allotted different river systems, while Chinese education was mainly in the hands of local school committees, organized by the Chinese themselves, who employed teachers from China.

Some imagination has been shown in tackling this difficult problem, though education has suffered seriously from lack of finance. Part of this is due to political considerations which will be discussed in the next chapter and part has resulted from the rajahs' policy of limited educational activity and low taxation.

There are several acute shortages which the development of education could help to relieve, but

[26] Consultative Committee on Economic Development in South and Southeast Asia, *The Colombo Plan*, 1956.

only if education were viewed not as a social service but as (at least in part) an instrument of development. There is virtually no technical training for artisans, the clerical services are extremely weak, and as a corollary of this there are very few able candidates for advanced technical training. But perhaps the greatest shortage is in agricultural extension work and the research on which this could be based. Some excellent social research has been done,[27] on the basis of which a great deal of extension work could have been undertaken, had the educated staff existed who could do this work. The lack of basic education has handicapped development in this field.

Sarawak is probably as fascinating a problem in economic development as Malaya. In some respects it seems more intractable, but one cannot resist the impression that there are many hopeful features, including considerable human and material resources. I should like to stimulate greater interest by American scholars and American foundations in the problems of this country. It seems to me that there are many respects in which the country could benefit economically from American experience and advice. It is American and not British experience that is relevant in developing by means of inland water transport a country which is short of labor. I find it difficult to believe that the problem of the Pelagus Ra-

[27] Morris, *Report on a . . . Community*; Freeman, *Iban Agriculture*; W. R. Geddes, *The Land Dyaks of Sarawak* (London: H. M. S. O., 1954) ; E. R. Leach, *Social Science Research in Sarawak* (London: H. M. S. O., 1950) ; Ju-K'ang T'ien, *The Chinese of Sarawak* (New York: Humanities Press, 1957).

pids, which has baffled local administrators for so
many years, could not be comparatively easily solved
by American engineers, so opening up to agriculture
and other development the huge area of the Upper
Rejang. I find it difficult to believe also that Americans would fail to find the community a sympathetic
one to assist. Many of the features of their social
organization which are rather uncongenial to British
ways of thinking would, I believe, be sympathetic to
Americans. At present there is no American con-
sulate in the country and American contacts are
through Singapore, which in Sibu seems almost as
far away as London.

An economist would be tempted to describe the
state of Brunei simply as an oil field. But such an
approach would neglect important demographic and
political factors that are extremely important for the
development of Northern Borneo as a whole. For
this small state with less than 100,000 people[28]
even now is the remnant of the power that was once
dominant throughout most of Borneo. The fact of
its former dominance is important for any consideration of political unity of the territory, since the people of the countries both to the northeast and the
southwest would regard it as something of a betrayal
to be forcibly reunited with Brunei, their former over-
lord. It is one of the ironies of this part of the world
that the Brookes, having first been given a small strip
of what is now Sarawak and having subsequently

[28] Brunei, *Annual Report, 1956* (Kuching: Government
Printer, 1957).

taken over more and more river systems from Brunei's control, should have left only this small Malay state with the comparatively independent status of a British-protected state, and that then nearly all the oil of Northern Borneo should be discovered within this territory.

The Sultan of Brunei is under British protection and the Governor of Sarawak is also High Commissioner for Brunei. In all important matters the Sultan is bound to ask and act upon the advice of the British Resident, who is a member of the Sarawak civil service. To most Americans and indeed to most Asian nationalists, the niceties of the distinction between colonial rule in Sarawak and North Borneo and British protection in Brunei might seem mere constitutional quibbles. In practice, however, the precise form of the relationship between Brunei, Sarawak, and the Colonial Office has had a tremendous influence on the development of the whole region. This is one of the topics with which I deal in the next chapter; here it is sufficient to point out that Brunei is very much an independent state in its relations with Sarawak, although the status of British protection does in fact involve complete control in all essentials by the colonial power.

The wealth from Brunei's oil is fantastic in relation to the population of the country. In some years the actual surplus of government revenue over expenditure has been equivalent to several hundred dollars a head for the whole indigenous population.[29]

Great developments have taken place in building and education since the Second World War, but the state remains extremely backward mainly because of shortage of labor for everything except production of oil. Because of the wealth it produces, the oil company is allowed to import most of the skilled labor it requires, though it is pursuing a progressive policy of training Brunei Malay labor wherever it can.

The transport system of Brunei is still rudimentary. Even now a part of the main road between the oil field and the capital of the state is simply a stretch of beach which can be negotiated by land-rovers and similar vehicles but not by ordinary cars.[30] The difficulty is not shortage of funds but acute shortage of labor combined with the remoteness of the area and some reluctance to spend money on a scale which the state could well afford. An example of this is the delay for several years in planning the main road because of the hope that the oil company would build a refinery near the capital and build its own road between that and the oil field.

Part of the revenues of the state have been used in financing a scheme of social security and social services, and something has been spent on improving local farming. Surveys have been attempted for possible fields of industrialization but so far with relatively little success.

[29] *Ibid.*   [30] *Ibid.*

The oil industry is allowed to import personnel both from Europe and from other Asian countries, and it does its best to give technical education to local children so as to build up a skilled labor force in Brunei itself.[31] The Brunei Malays are opposed to immigration of Chinese except for specific requirements in the oil industry, but it seems unlikely that Brunei Malay labor will ever suffice for the oil industry's needs. Iban from Sarawak come in on temporary permits, and their experience in working in the oil industry could be potentially much more educative than that of the timber industry of Sarawak. Opposition from both the Brunei and Sarawak governments has so far prevented any considerable settlement of Iban for advanced technical training, though some show considerable mechanical aptitude.

In the early postwar years the oil industry of Brunei was obliged to undertake most of the essential services for its labor force. In recent years it has been trying increasingly to hand over its functions in transport, distribution, building, and the like to any local entrepreneurs who seem likely to be able to do the work.

In spite of the poor transport systems in Brunei and Sarawak, unskilled labor of the pagan peoples is surprisingly mobile. A decline in sago production induces large numbers of Melanaus to travel up the coast to work in the oil fields. Iban labor is mobile because it is part of the culture pattern of these people for the young men to go on a journey

[31] Brunei, *Annual Report, 1956.*

for a few months every year. These workers who come from very primitive settlements would appear to offer an exciting prospect for community development work, though hitherto this has not been undertaken among the migrant labor in the Brunei area.

The colony of North Borneo was administered right up to the Second World War by a chartered company mainly engaged in the extraction of timber. It suffered far heavier damage during the war than the rest of Borneo and for years its rehabilitation was a burden on the British Treasury.[32] Like the other two territories, it suffers acutely from shortage of labor, and this has greatly hampered reconstruction and the development of transport. The physical engineering difficulties of constructing roads are considerably less in North Borneo than elsewhere, but the colony is much poorer and has little capital of its own to develop a good road system. The interior is also less well served by rivers than that of Sarawak, which makes a road system more of a necessity.

The problem has been tackled with some vigor. A number of bridle paths from prewar times are being improved to carry jeep traffic, and earth roads are being built to open up new areas, with frank recognition that these roads will not be usable all the year round.

Chinese have been settled for many generations in Borneo, and there has been intermarriage with some of the local peoples. Probably this has stimulated a

[32] North Borneo, *Annual Reports, 1947-55* (Jesselton: Government Printing Department, 1950-1955).

willingness to accept changing ways of life. There is less pressure of population on the lands where shifting cultivation is practiced, partly because of a decline in numbers of the Murut tribe, which may however be itself a result of some of them abandoning shifting cultivation and ceasing to count themselves as Muruts. This in turn has resulted in making the government sympathetic to new planting of rubber. There has also been a good deal of success in encouraging other opening up of new lands by small farmers.

The economy rests on rubber, timber, and copra, and the trade of the entrepôt ports. North Borneo's planting conditions being rather similar to those of Malaya, it has been possible to secure a good deal of help from the Rubber Research Institute of Malaya, and interest in high-yielding material is widespread. Most of the area planted with high-yielding varieties is new planting, which has made it easier for smallholders to take a predominant part in this development.

Timber was, before the Second World War, the most important product extracted by the British North Borneo Company. Some years after the war its successor, the British Borneo Timber Company, by agreement with the government, gave up its monopoly of Borneo's timber trade. During the past seven years cutting has expanded rapidly, particularly by small companies operating on short-term licenses. In 1955 regulations were introduced restricting this trade, mainly with a view to maintaining conservative forestry practice, but also to keep prices from falling further as a result of low-cost competition.

As a result of considerable public feeling, expressed in the press, the government has negotiated long-term leases with the leading local timber companies and has agreed to consider similar leases for the smaller companies. The effect, however, will inevitably be to raise costs.

It is open to question whether a country as empty as North Borneo could not afford rather more wasteful forestry methods for the sake of fostering a group of small entrepreneurs, some of whom might well be expected to reinvest their profits in developing new trade and new crops. Conservative forestry practices need large amounts of capital and large-scale operation, and small capitalists may well be a more valuable asset than the forest estate which they consume.

The whole subject of forest reservation is one that merits more economic consideration. It must be conceded that a long view should be taken and that external economies may be considerable. The economic advantage from preserving a forest may, for example, greatly exceed the forest products to be derived from it if its existence prevents soil erosion or flooding on neighboring agricultural land. But a forestry department should, in a free economy, pay an economic rent for any potential agricultural or mining land which it uses purely for the production of timber and other forest products, unless a forest is really needed there for protective purposes. And because it is in part a business enterprise with interests of its own, it should normally be required to defend its claims for land for conservation purposes against the claims for other national interests, before an independent authority.

Like Sarawak, North Borneo is badly handicapped in its development by lack of basic education. The government has, however, responded more effectively to the keenness of the indigenous population, so that the racial balance of North Borneo's education is better than that of Sarawak. The percentage of the total population in school in North Borneo is slightly lower, and neither country has a clear estimate of the population of school age.

In neighboring countries, two of North Borneo's ports have attracted some interest and speculation: the island of Labuan, which regained its free port status in 1956, and the small but rapidly developing entrepôt port of Tawau.

Labuan before the war was the smallest of the four settlements known as the Straits Settlements and was a free port serving the territories of Northern Borneo. The territories which it served were not particularly prosperous, and it remained a small center of purely local trade. It is now, however, a port in close proximity to the wealthy territory of Brunei, and its airport is a potential international center for air traffic.

Speculation is often heard among merchants concerning the possibility of much of the entrepôt trade of Singapore being transferred to Labuan as a result of political developments in Malaya. There seems in fact very little chance that this will occur. Not only is Brunei developing its own ocean port across the bay from Labuan, but there is also a serious problem of labor shortage. North Borneo, which now administers Labuan, has been persuaded to restore its free-port status but is unlikely to look with favor on large-scale immigration of Chinese labor from Singapore or Hong Kong.

Of even greater interest are developments that are taking place in Tawau, which is rapidly developing into an important center both of smuggling and of legitimate trade with neighboring territories in both Indonesia and the Philippines. Although it does not enjoy free-port status, it is an area of relative stability and freedom from control, attracting to itself the trade that is trying to escape from vexatious but ineffective regulation. In this it is following the traditions of Singapore which grew by breaking the commercial monopoly of the Dutch in the early nineteenth century. Indeed geography has enabled Tawau to follow this tradition of a center of relative freedom becoming an entrepôt for surrounding areas better than Labuan, in spite of the latter's free-port status.

This brings us to consideration of the three great entrepôt ports—Penang, Singapore, and Hong Kong —which are the real centers of the Commonwealth economy of the area.

Although the patterns of trade of Penang and Singapore are similar, there are important differences resulting from both location and political status. Both ports engage in entrepôt trade in rubber, tin, timber, copra, areca nuts, and various other kinds of Straits produce, and both distribute industrial products shipped from all over the world to minor ports in the neighborhood.[33] Singapore, however, was the capital of the old Straits Settlements and in effect the economic and political capital of Malaya before the war, and was a collecting and distributing center for a much larger area than Penang. The separation of Singapore as a separate political entity and the inclusion of Penang within the Federation of Malaya have not operated to destroy this advantage of Singapore but, for the present at least, to accentuate it.

For a few months after the end of the war Penang actually lost its free-port status and was brought within the customs area of the Federation of Malaya.[34] Later, the free-port status of Penang Island was restored, while the remainder of the former settlement remained within the customs area. Discussions are still proceeding about the desirability of bringing Penang Island back within the Federation customs areas for import duties, but not for export duties, and providing Penang with special storage facilities for the entrepôt trade.[35] New economic development

[33] T. H. Silcock, *The Economy of Malaya* (Singapore: Donald Moore, 1954); Straits Settlements, *Commission Appointed by H. E. the Governor to Enquire into and Report on the Trade of the Colony: Report* (Singapore: Government Printer, 1934).

[34] F. C. C. Benham, *Report on the Trade of Penang* (Kuala Lumpur: Government Printer, 1948).

[35] Federation of Malaya, *Report of the Penang Customs Duties Working Party* (Kuala Lumpur: Government Printer, 1957).

has not been attracted to Penang as it has to Singapore, partly perhaps because of the feeling among the wealthy Chinese of Southeast Asia that the interests of Penang are likely to be subordinated to those of the Federation of Malaya, which is mainly a producer of primary products, while the trade of Singapore remains one of the chief concerns of its government.

Penang's entrepôt trade is with Sumatra (and particularly with the Northern Province of Atjeh) and also with South Burma and South Thailand, which are rather isolated regions with no close contact with the capitals of the two countries. It also handles most of the trade of Northern Malaya. Unlike Singapore, however, it has no range of islands and river basins at all comparable with the string of islands stretching away towards Borneo and Java or the river systems of Borneo itself. It is an entrepôt port serving outlying regions of three foreign countries, and its role in this respect has been weakened by the transfer of sovereign control from Singapore, which had similar interests, to Kuala Lumpur. It will probably, however, continue to derive a good deal of revenue from entrepôt trade with these regions, particularly as such entrepôt trade flourishes better with weak governments than with strong ones. There is no great probability that neighboring countries will cease to try to secure more autarky in their economic affairs, but so long as their power of exercising economic control is weak such efforts will favor rather than hamper the position of Penang.

Penang's industry is mainly confined to processing

a few of the region's products, for example, tin smelting, coconut oil production, rubber milling, and a little saw-milling. Such industrialization as there is, is mainly on the island, in the free-port area, where it can use both Malayan and foreign materials, rather than on the mainland. Indeed the oil mills on the island have largely taken the business away from the small local mills[36] which developed during and after the war in the North of the mainland, in spite of an unfavorable export duty on Malayan copra. This concentration on the island, however, means that Penang's industries will not benefit from any protective legislation introduced by an independent Malaya unless the island is included. If there is any transfer of industry from Singapore, it seems more likely to move to the small but growing industrial center in the neighborhood of Kuala Lumpur.

Singapore as an entrepôt center has all the advantages of Penang, but many others in addition. It has a much larger range of small local ports, from which transshipment is necessary if international trade with the rest of the world is to take place. In addition, however, it is a convenient regional center for overseas businesses operating throughout the Far Eastern area. There is much talk at present of businesses transferring their Malayan headquarters from Singapore to Kuala Lumpur, but they are unlikely to transfer their headquarters for Eastern Asia away

[36] Information derived from an Honors Graduation Exercise presented by S. Selvadurai to the University of Malaya, July, 1957, but unpublished.

from Singapore. In its early days Singapore was the entrepôt center for trade from as far away as the China coast and the island of Celebes. Since that time there has been some increase in direct shipment from ocean ports elsewhere in the region and particularly from Hong Kong. But the great speed and ease of transport has made it convenient for many firms to maintain a headquarters in Singapore covering areas that often stretch almost as far as those which it served during its first twenty years.

Singapore has also built up the leading organized produce markets in the whole region. Its market for rubber handles more of the trade than any other market in the world.[37] Its market for Straits produce sets the grades and prices for most of the produce of the region. It has also an active stock market. The commercial *expertise* and technical knowledge associated with these markets are an important source of wealth to Singapore, and their presence in one place reinforces the tendency of Singapore to serve as a natural economic capital for the whole Southeast Asian region.

Separate national income figures were not published for Singapore before 1957, though there was a brief discussion of the question in a *Report on Minimum Standards of Livelihood*.[38] It is possible to break down a fair proportion of Dr. Benham's

[37] Joan Wilson, *The Singapore Rubber Market* (Singapore: Donald Moore, 1958).
[38] Singapore, *Committee on Minimum Standards of Livelihood Report* (Singapore: Government Printer, 1957).

figures on the national income of Malaya,[39] and this indicates that in the early postwar years approximately one-third of the income was concentrated in Singapore, with only about one-sixth of the population. More recent evidence, particularly the 1957 *Economic Survey of Singapore*,[40] suggests that the proportion of the income of Malaya accruing in Singapore may have declined a little, while the proportion of its population has increased during the last decade. It is still unlikely, however, that Singapore's income per head is much less than double that of the Federation. Bearing in mind that Malaya has, with the possible exception of Israel and Hong Kong, the highest income per head in Asia, the prosperity of Singapore needs no futher emphasis. It is almost certainly the only place in Asia where there is a really substantial middle class with a standard of living as high as that of most of Europe. With more than one car for every thirty people, Singapore's million and a half people have more than one-tenth as many cars as the total of India, Japan, Indonesia, and Pakistan, with more than four hundred times Singapore's population.[41]

It is probable that the revenue from the entrepôt trade of Singapore has been increasing during the postwar decade as a result of the comparative weakening of the government of Indonesia. Much of this

[39] F. C. C. Benham, *National Income of Malaya, 1947-1949* (Singapore: Government Printer, 1951).

[40] F. C. C. Benham, *Economic Survey of Singapore* (Singapore: Government Printer, 1957).

[41] UNECAFE, *Economic Survey* (1956).

trade is of a more or less irregular nature, so that statistics are unreliable and also difficult to interpret. Indonesia has been trying to restrict the flow of trade to Singapore,[42] and its efforts have had some success in limiting from time to time the import of smallholders' rubber for milling in Singapore. There is, however, a very extensive black market in Indonesian currency and it is probable that the margins of profit on business done with that country are ample to compensate for any decline in volume.

This comparatively favorable picture should not be interpreted as a forecast of continuing prosperity. There are several threatening features in Singapore's situation which lead one to doubt whether the present high standards can be maintained. If the Indonesian government remains unable to control its economy effectively, the long-run decline of prosperity, while strengthening Singapore's relative position, must ultimately weaken the whole region. On the other hand, if Indonesia increases in prosperity, it may well succeed in the end in diverting much of the trade of the outlying islands to Djakarta and other Indonesian ports.

Both Sarawak and Brunei are attempting to develop their own ocean ports, and although a single main port of call in the region, with transshipment into small ships, is likely to remain as the pattern for many minor products, some of the major items of

[42] Singapore, Department of Commerce and Industry, *Report*, 1955.

Singapore trade may be diverted when the larger ocean-going ships can call elsewhere.

The Federation of Malaya has also developed a very critical attitude toward the economic role of Singapore, which it tends to regard as a feature of the colonialism which Malaya has outgrown. Undoubtedly, this will lead to increasing attempts to divert the Federation's trade to ports within the Federation itself. This could do some damage to Singapore, but a greater threat is the attempt to establish a separate currency and banking system and to establish in Kuala Lumpur the organized produce markets and head office business that are at present found in Singapore.

There is, of course, no serious danger of this policy succeeding. The position of Singapore depends partly on geography, partly on the trade connections of the Chinese of Southeast Asia, and partly on commercial skills which the Federation's policy is most unlikely to attract to Kuala Lumpur. The danger is rather that measures taken against Singapore will provoke political retaliation and so generate increasing interference with the trade between the two areas. For although the Federation could certainly not attract much of Singapore's business to Kuala Lumpur, it could by weakening Singapore as a commercial center drive some of the business away from Malaya altogether. Nor is it possible to confine consideration of this problem solely to its economic aspect. If there is one thing that has been apparent in Malaya ever since the war, it is that the very existence of the country depends on winning over an appreciable proportion of the Chinese to give their first loyalty to Malaya. By excluding Singapore the Malays can retain their majority long enough to give them a chance to absorb a proportion of the Chinese instead of being swamped by a united Chinese majority. It is possible, though not easy, to win Malaya's Chinese wholly away from Communist China so long as most Singapore Chinese are prepared to acquiesce in the position of political separation.[43] But any serious decline in Singapore's prosperity could rapidly convert it into an active center of leadership and supplies for a renewed terrorist movement, and such terrorism might then command the support of a far higher proportion of the Chinese in Malaya than the Communists have so far been able to command.

Probably the temporary separation of the Federation and Singapore offers the best chance of successful political development. But if the Federation regards any decision-making in Singapore, even in commercial matters, as a relic of colonialism to be destroyed, while Singapore regards any attempt to modify the economic system as a proof of Malay anti-Chinese bias, the situation could rapidly deteriorate.

This is the situation in which Singapore has to cope with a rate of population increase of over 3½ per cent per annum. Some 10-15 per cent of the

[43] T. H. Silcock, *Dilemma in Malaya* (Research Series, No. 135) (London: Fabian Colonial Bureau, 1948); "Forces for Unity in Malaya," *International Affairs*, XXV (1949), 453-465.

national income needs to be invested to prevent a decline in capital equipment per head. Nearly half the population is under twenty, and further gigantic efforts are needed to prevent the average level of education from declining. In both these respects Singapore seems to be doing slightly better than is necessary to prevent deterioration; but if the entrepôt trade is to decline, or at least not increase, Singapore will have to industrialize very rapidly to maintain its existing standards.

A good deal is being done in this respect with the development of technical education, establishment of industrial estates by public enterprise, and more recently by the development of special institutions to stimulate both the financing and the development of local industry.[44] Singapore wages are high by Asian standards, and this means both high capitalization and high levels of productivity if Singapore is to compete with its Asian rivals in producing industrial goods.

Industrial skills in Singapore have been built up partly by the presence of the naval base and the Harbour Board with its ship-repairing services, partly by repair work, and later by assembly of cars and trucks. There are factories making small products like batteries and shoe polish and also the usual textile mills, breweries, and soft-drink factories. The

[44] Singapore, *Annual Report, 1956* (Singapore: Government Printer, 1957); T. H. Silcock, "Probleme der Staatlichen Unabhängigheit in Südostasien," in *Studien zur Entwicklung in Südost und Ostasien*, Instituts für Asienkunde, Hamburg, 1958.

International Bank in its recent *Report on Malaya*[45] emphasized the existing prevalence of small-scale industries producing a wide range of products and advocated measures to encourage their growth both in size and in number.

Finding a market may present a serious problem here, since Singapore has no large market of its own and cannot compete by the use of cheap labor. It seems imperative, therefore, that Singapore should acquire and retain a technical lead in the development of new products and processes in the Southeast Asian region. The existing high standards in the local market and the prevalence of local capital and enterprise should make this possible, but difficulties are likely to be encountered in fitting the most advanced technical processes, which depend on functional specialization, into the pattern of traditional Chinese business which is the basis of most local enterprise.

The methods by which the existing Chinese-owned enterprises have developed, and also the ways in which capital formation has been carried on, will one day be fascinating fields for economic research.

Hong Kong is industrially far ahead of Singapore, though its standard of living is considerably lower.[46] Hong Kong was faced nearly ten years ago with the

[45] International Bank for Reconstruction and Development, *Economic Development of Malaya* (Baltimore: Johns Hopkins Press, 1955).

[46] R. A. Ma and E. F. Szczepanik, *National Income of Hong Kong* (London: Oxford University Press, 1955); F. C. C. Benham, *Economic Survey of Singapore* (Singapore: Government Printer, 1957); and "The Growth of Manufacturing in Hong Kong," *International Affairs*, XXXII (1956), 456-463.

problems of a dwindling entrepôt trade in a territory where relatively high standards had already developed on the basis of more than a century as a trade center for South China. It enjoyed, however, considerable advantages in comparison with Singapore in capital, labor, and, above all, enterprise. Many Shanghai capitalists succeeded in transferring funds to Hong Kong for industrial development before Shanghai fell into Communist hands. A large and rapidly growing refugee population has maintained a supply of both skilled and unskilled labor and kept wages low in relation to productivity. Above all among the refugees from China, many are traders and small capitalists who have introduced an ample supply of eager entrepreneurs.

On this basis Hong Kong, without either raw materials or a market of its own, has built up a very substantial degree of industrialization and is tackling with some success the problem of coping with its large refugee population. A firm government pursuing a liberal policy in relation to trade, a stable currency linked to sterling but with a system of exchange control much more liberal than any other in the sterling area,[47] and a well-developed system of education have given it further advantages.

Although much of Hong Kong's former entrepôt trade with China has been lost since the Revolution and the Korean War, Hong Kong still maintains important entrepôt functions with neighboring territo-

[47] "Monetary Systems of the Colonies," *The Banker*, LXXXVII (1948), 33-39.

ries. One interesting branch of trade is the entrepôt trade in dollar goods to Malaya and Singapore, and via Singapore to other places in Southeast Asia.

From the beginnings of sterling area exchange control, in the early days of the war, Hong Kong has enjoyed a special position in relation to the sterling area by virtue of its entrepôt trade. In Singapore it was possible to make special regulations for the entrepôt trade without relaxing the fundamental rules of the sterling area. In Hong Kong, however, most of the entrepôt trade would have left Hong Kong altogether if all dollar proceeds had had to be surrendered. This was the origin of the system of allowing Hong Kong traders to retain a proportion of their own dollar earnings and hence also the origin of the free currency market in Hong Kong. It is by the possession of dollars acquired from one of these two sources that Hong Kong residents are able to buy dollar goods, for which permits would not be granted in Malaya, and to re-export them to Malaya.

This is a feature of the sterling area exchange control system in the region which seems to have caused a good deal of confusion. I have often been asked whether this represents connivance at a breach of sterling area regulations and, if not, what advantage there can be either to Malaya or the sterling area in allowing dollar goods to enter at high prices via Hong Kong when their direct entry is restricted.

This is an *ad hoc* arrangement which benefits the sterling area control system rather than working to its disadvantage. Without the special Hong Kong concession for exports to the dollar area, fewer dollars would be earned through Hong Kong's trade. But once the free dollars are in the hands of Hong Kong merchants, it is eminently desirable from a sterling area point of view that these dollars should be used to buy luxury goods for import into Malaya rather than used for the export of capital from the sterling area. The chief point at which Hong Kong is dangerous to the sterling area system is its possibility of serving as a loop-hole for capital flight, since the sterling area rules normally provide for free movement of capital within the area. In practice there is a good deal of control over capital remittances by sterling area residents into Hong Kong so as to plug this leak. The use of free dollars for bringing luxuries into Malaya is a lesser evil and helps to lessen inflationary pressure in Malaya because some of these goods would have been permitted and would have been a drain on the dollar pool.

This completes the brief sketch of the economies within the Commonwealth system, though a brief reference must be made to Burma, which is geographically within the region and economically linked to the Commonwealth system, although the links are becoming increasingly tenuous.

When it decided to leave the Commonwealth on achieving independence, Burma retained its tariff system based on Imperial Preference and its link with the sterling area. Events of subsequent years appear to indicate that this was more a result of administrative difficulties in suddenly transforming the economy than a deliberate policy of maintaining economic links while destroying the political ones. The Imperial Preference tariff system has now been abandoned, but during the period of high prices of rice, which lasted until 1954, the sterling area link seemed wholly to Burma's advantage, giving it an easy clearing system and continued access to short-term capital from London.

The kyat, however, has now become a very weak currency as a result of deterioration in the rice market and of Burma's determination to carry through its development plans in spite of weakening reserves and the need for heavy military expenditure. The weakness is severely aggravated by local capital flight, especially among Indian traders in Burma. This has made it necessary for Burma to impose strict additional exchange controls that go far beyond those of most of the sterling area. Freedom of capital movement from the rest of the sterling area into Burma has materially declined in importance as a result of these restrictions, so that the sterling area link has now become little more than a clearing system. As a clearing system, however, it is probably still a source of strength to the kyat, especially against non-Asian currencies, and a material help toward the purchase of capital equipment. If Burma were to abandon the sterling link, it would probably encounter much greater difficulties in controlling capital flight, since it certainly would find it difficult to

pay for its capital imports on a bilateral basis. T
the economic links are still of some importance,
it is probably hardly realistic to regard Burma a
still part of the Commonwealth economic system.

2

The Commonwealth Impact

IN THIS CHAPTER I propose to discuss the economic impact of the British system of political development from colonial or protected status into membership of the Commonwealth on the economy of the Southeast Asian region. It is difficult for an Englishman to look at this system of development from outside and survey its favorable and unfavorable points impartially, but that is what I shall aim to do. First, then, I should like to indicate some of the general characteristics of this system which I propose to explore in detail.

The most obvious characteristic is an absence of general principle, or even of a general policy, uniformly imposed, as far as possible, on all dependent territories. Power has been acquired for a variety of purposes and not usually even with a consistent policy at headquarters but rather through the acts of local officials responding to local situations. Probably the most frequent motive has been the desire to remedy specific local abuses, sometimes but not always as a result of threats to existing British trading or territorial interests.

Because there has been no consistent motive for the acquisition of power, there has been no uniform policy of control and no deliberate line of advance toward self-government. In the Southeast Asian area, this has had favorable and unfavorable effects on development through the political structures that it has built up and the economic institutions that it has caused to develop.

A second important feature of the British Commonwealth system is the emergence of separate classes of officials and traders with special interests of their own distinct from those of both the home country and the local territory.[1] The relative strength of these different groups and the setting in which either government or business has to be carried on have had a great influence on the nature of development in each place through their reaction on the outlook of these small but important groups. Englishmen are prepared to live abroad for long periods, often for most of their working life, but do not in general settle in the countries to which they go or intermarry with the inhabitants. This is a most unusual system, and it has been much commoner in the past for power to be exercised either through a class which settles and intermarries, ultimately becoming a ruling caste within the country, or through officials whose residence is comparatively brief.

[1] J. S. Furnivall, *Colonial Policy and Practice* (Cambridge: Cambridge University Press, 1948).

A third feature related to the other two is the tendency to develop special institutions related to economic needs and based on some adaptation of institutions in the home country to local conditions. These institutions are not generally clearly related to any long-run plan of development but have often been highly successful in tackling the problems which they confronted. It could be argued that British institutions owe their survival to a basic cultural pattern favorable to flexibility and adaptation, and that it would be contrary to the whole character of British thought to attempt to design institutions for development in a particular direction. This is a sound point, but if there was a hope that flexible self-governing institutions would ultimately develop, one might have expected a more deliberate policy of reproducing the cultural conditions in which such flexibility would naturally grow. Instead, the system actually adopted has been one that encourages flexibility and enterprise only at the last minute and in emergency conditions. There are signs that the challenge is being met, but it is difficult to resist the impression that a method of political development suitable for colonies populated by people with British traditions and outlook has been rather rashly grafted on to colonies with different local traditions and with a more urgent need for social change and rapid development.

The successful economic developments in the region of Southeast Asia have almost all been results of *ad hoc* political solutions of local problems. The entrepôt trade of Penang was an almost incidental result of the strategic need for a naval station on the eastern shore of the Bay of Bengal. Singapore, admittedly, was a deliberate product of the vision of Stamford Raffles, who saw just such an entrepôt port at the crossroads of Southeast Asia when he arranged his deal with the Temenggong (ruler) of Johore. Certainly the development of European tin mining and the opening up of the country by the rubber industry were not envisaged when the policy of appointing advisers in the Malay States was adopted. There was a local desire to develop the hinterland adjoining the Straits Settlements and to control the dangers to the trading activities of British subjects resulting from feuds among gangs of Chinese miners or strife between the different sultans. The revenue from tin mining was used to develop roads and railways, and it was only after this that the rubber boom led to rapid development of most of the west coast. European tin mining did not compete successfully with the Chinese methods until the introduction of tin dredges just before and after the First World War.[2]

The rapid development of the tin and rubber industries led to the emergence of the Federated Malay States, which was administered virtually as a colony. The indigenous institutions were those of the constituent states, and the fact that they were preserved and used for the administration of the local peasants is significant for later development. All

[2] Sir Lewis L. Fermor, *Report on the Mining Industry of Malaya* (Kuala Lumpur: Government Printer, 1940).

the main administrative work for the economic development of Malaya's major industries was done by the Federal Administration in which the sultans and the state governments had very little influence.

It should be noted that it was not the deliberate policy of the Federated Malay States government to develop the smallholders' rubber industry which now occupies such an important position in Malaya's economy. The desertion by the Malays of their rice fields and the planting of a commercial crop like rubber was in general viewed with alarm both by the sultans' governments and by their British advisers. The policy of reserving large areas of land in the Malay States to prevent their transfer to non-Malay ownership appears to have been designed mainly to prevent encroachment by other races into rice farming and to preserve the Malays in their traditional agricultural practices.

The Federation government was concerned with all the administrative activities involved in opening up new economic areas, controlling the treatment of immigrant labor, and insuring the basic conditions of health and security.

Forty years ago the emergence of a strong central government designed for the economic development of Malaya might well have been regarded as inevitable. The Federated Malay States and the Straits Settlements had only to assimilate the State of Johore (already under British protection) to create a solid and united territory from Penang to Singapore to which the other four Malay States would have been virtually bound to accede with the passage of time.

In 1925, however, there was a reaction from this tendency designed to concentrate in Singapore the essential economic power for fostering the development of the country, while restoring the system of indirect rule through the Malay sultans.

The policy, announced by the Governor, Sir Laurence Guillemard, was one of weakening the Federation and raising the status of the individual state governments. This policy encountered considerable opposition and was introduced only gradually, the final stage being implemented only after the visit to Malaya of the Under-Secretary of State for the Colonies, Sir Samuel Wilson, in 1932.

To understand this it is necessary to recall the position of the British advisers in the different Malay States.[3] Although the essential powers of control had been given by treaty to the British administration, the form of control was that of advice to a Mohammedan monarch. The sultans and their Malay advisers in the unfederated states could hardly be expected to welcome the concentration of administrative decisions in all Federal matters in the capital at Kuala Lumpur and the reduction of the sultans' governments in the federated states to little more than local governments with ceremonial and religious func-

[3] S. W. Jones, *Public Administration in Malaya* (New York and London: Royal Institute of International Affairs, 1953); Lennox A. Mills, *British Rule in Eastern Asia* (Minneapolis: University of Minnesota Press, 1942); R. Emerson, *Malaysia* (New York: Macmillan, 1937).

tions. Moreover, the development of the economy of the country by immigrant labor was leaving the Malays economically backward in a rich country, and the administrators who were formally assisting Malay rulers felt some concern to set a limit to this tendency.

A process of decentralizing authority to the individual Malay states seemed to hold out the hope of increasing possibilities of centralization, through Pan-Malayan departments in Singapore, of essential economic functions, while allaying the suspicions and fears of the governments of the unfederated states and strengthening the defenses of the Malay peasants and the Malay aristocracy against too rapid economic development. The divergence of interest between the business community and the government was not absolute, but the decentralization policy represented a partial attempt to curb the influence of the business community.

This policy of decentralization sowed the seeds both of hostility between Kuala Lumpur and Singapore and of jealousy by the state governments of Federal powers. The European and non-Malay business interests of the Federated Malay States interpreted the policy both as a threat to their interests by Singapore and as a reaction in favor of the Malays, and these feelings were important in the postwar reconstruction.

After the war an attempt was made to draw up a new constitution in which all the Malay States and the Settlements of Penang and Malacca would be united while Singapore would remain a separate political entity. This plan was drawn up in London in the expectation that Malaya would be reconquered with active assistance from Chinese guerillas, while the Malay States governments would be put in the position of having co-operated with the Japanese against them. A sudden end of the war was not foreseen in the planning unit—one of the incidental results of the secrecy surrounding the preparation of the atomic bomb.[4]

The actual circumstances in which the British returned to Malaya favored greater continuity, and the Malayan union was not supported either by the Malays, who regarded it as an attack on their rights, or by the non-Malays, who saw it as insufficiently democratic. The Federation Constitution ultimately negotiated favored the Malays, and the way in which it did so was to strengthen the powers of the states against the Federation and to base the Federation government partly on citizenship to which non-Malays would have some access and partly on state representation, leaving the states almost wholly in Malay hands.

As a result of these developments, both the separation of Singapore from the Federation and the preservation of state rights have become matters on which racial feelings can easily be aroused, and change is therefore difficult.

The decentralization policy before the war was

[4] T. H. Silcock and U. A. Aziz, *Nationalism in Malaya* (New York: Institute of Pacific Relations, 1950).

intended to unite and not to divide the basic economic structure of Malaya, and it did in fact have that effect. Neither the Malayan Union plan nor the Federation Agreement aimed at breaking up this unified economy. They have, however, tended to produce that effect in two respects. The separation of Singapore from the Federation has strengthened both Singapore and Kuala Lumpur at the expense of Penang and has also led to a highly dangerous situation for future development of the whole economy. The delegation of important powers to the states has hampered development both of agriculture and of mining and may well cause serious effects when the unifying influence of a British civil service is removed. These two points will now be developed in more detail.

The immediate postwar policies were not, as has been indicated, characterized by a high level of economic intelligence. Not only was it at first seriously intended to bring Penang within the customs union and so effectively destroy any prospect of restoring its prewar entrepôt trade. It was apparently also envisaged that hostility between the Federation of Malaya and Singapore could be indefinitely fostered without damaging the economic co-operation on which the welfare of both so obviously depends. The separation of the two territories, accompanied by deliberate stirring up of business rivalries, has now led many of the Malays in the Federation to regard the economic control by Singapore as one of the relics of colonialism which an independent Malaya must try to break. In Singapore, on the other hand, the unwillingness of the Federation government to accept Singapore into the Federation has been accepted without very bitter opposition only because it is believed to be a purely temporary concession. It is felt that independence in Malaya will not be complete until the separation, which is attributed to British influence, has been brought to an end. Consequently, any attempts by the Federation government to separate the economies of the two territories is likely to meet with strong resentment.

Issues on which immediate disagreement is likely would include the constitution of the Central Bank[5] and the imposition of protective tariffs to foster Federation industries to the detriment of Singapore. In both these matters the attitude of the Federation has so far gone about as far as it is reasonable to expect in view of the current political feeling. The Federation does not appear to be pressing for a separate Central Bank but rather to be intending to establish its own Central Bank and allow Singapore to join it. If Singapore were prepared to accept this, the relationship that would develop would presumably be rather like that between Washington and New York in the United States system; and the real tension would be deferred until policy issues arose in which there might be a conflict between them. In trade, the Federation is taking the line that it cannot under the rules of the General Agreement on Tariffs and

[5] P. W. Sherwood, "The Watson-Caine Report on the Establishment of a Central Bank in Malaya," *Malayan Economic Review*, II, No. 1 (April, 1957), 23-34.

Trade grant special tariff concessions to Singapore; that it must be free to impose tariffs to foster any industrialization which can be expected to take place within the Federation; but that it is prepared to consult with Singapore about the general tariffs to be imposed.

To Singapore politicians it seems at present entirely unreasonable for the Central Bank to be located anywhere else than in Singapore, where much the greatest volume of banking is done.[6] Moreover, it is regarded as spiteful for the Federation to try to attract into its own territory industries which are already established within Malaya on the island of Singapore.

There should be no difficulty in working out a policy which would divert to the Federation a few manufactures that Singapore could spare and that would give the Federation rather more control than Singapore over the policy of a combined Central Bank. This would be a reasonable compromise in view of the fact that the Federation is now the major partner in an economy which cannot be split without harm to both sides. The difficulty will be to persuade Singapore merchants and politicians that such a policy is in fact reasonable. For many who accept political separation as a necessary and presumably temporary evil, the economic consequences of the separation will seem as ridiculous as they do to any economist. Yet, with the prevailing Malay attitude to Singapore as

[6] International Bank for Reconstruction and Development, *The Economic Development of Malaya* (Baltimore: Johns Hopkins, 1955).

only one remove from the colonial power, it is impossible to hope for anything better. Indeed, the probable consequence is something very much worse, namely, increasing mutual irritation over tariffs and financial policy, causing economic harm to both, and in both undermining political stability.

This situation was largely the result of the policy of the first postwar High Commissioner of the Federation, Sir Edward Gent.[7] The separation of Singapore from the Malayan Union had been largely his policy,[8] and he appears to have focussed the business jealousies of Kuala Lumpur, the anti-Chinese feelings of the Malay aristocracy, and the ambitions of the civil service into hostility to Singapore. Granted the basic policy of separation, this would fulfil the threefold objective of giving a sense of unity to the new Federation, canalizing anti-Chinese feeling outside the Federation itself, and keeping Singapore in British hands. The economic consequences appear to have been either ignored or treated as unimportant.

It is not here suggested that there was no natural Malay opposition to the commercial power of Singapore. It is by no means unnatural that the Malays, who have been largely left behind in a country where they once were a majority of the population, should

[7] No proper study has yet been made of this brilliant and controversial administrator. The views here expressed are based not on research, but on residence in Malaya at the time and fairly extensive discussions both in Kuala Lumpur and in Singapore, undertaken with a view to preparing a memorandum on the subject to the Colonial Office.

[8] Information based on discussions with members of the wartime Malaya Planning Unit.

be jealous of the immigrants who have made money in their country. But the consequences of this local device to strengthen the cohesion of the Federation are perhaps the most striking examples of the weakness of proceeding by political improvisation.

We turn next to the problems that have arisen from the Federation Agreement. It was probably sound policy and in line with previous British practice to meet the unforeseen strength of Malay resistance to the Malayan Union by strengthening the powers of the state governments. It was probably assumed that this would build into the Constitution some safeguard for Malay rights without seriously weakening the co-ordinating power of the Federation government. The sultans' governments in the states had been staffed partly by Malay aristocrats with little technical training and partly by British civil servants who were under the control of the Establishment Office and of their technical heads in Singapore or Kuala Lumpur. The original Federation Agreement could hardly have been considered workable unless state functions had in fact been reasonably co-ordinated by a European civil service.

The statement that the Federation Agreement did not imply genuinely independent action by the states does not mean that decentralization was only a political gesture. The fact that land policy and the administration of education, for example, were left to the states could be expected to influence policy in these two fields by insuring that the Headquarters Department would have to carry state governments with it and not merely the Federal secretariat. This would mean that Malay interests would carry more weight than they would have done in a purely central form of government. There was some possibility of an ambitious state education officer playing the state government off against his own technical chief in Kuala Lumpur but generally he could be relied on to treat the Federal Director of Education as his chief, and most British civil servants, liable for transfer between different states every few years and dependent for recognition chiefly on the recommendations of the Federal department head, would similarly be relied on to carry out his policies within the practical limits of the local political setting.

The immediate economic effect of the Federation Agreement was not, therefore, to break up the economy by encouraging independent state policies. It is much more significant that the administration in the states has been a good deal weaker than that of the Federal government.

To understand the reason for this, it is necessary to see the state governments in relation to the existing educational planning. At the time of the Federation Agreement these state governments were still very largely the secretariats of Muslim sultans and were staffed very largely by Malays, with a fairly high proportion of members of the politically influential families. Many of them were very weak in educated and qualified personnel. An attempt was, however, made after the war to insist on formal qualifications and to build up the administrative strength of these governments. But the senior officers still remain almost wholly Malay or British.

It must be understood that very few able and educated Malays are available for staffing the Federal and state civil services. The Malays are predominantly a rural people and until about the Second World War they strongly mistrusted Western education. A high proportion of education at the secondary level was in the hands of Christian missions, which encountered far less opposition from Chinese and Indians than from the Muslim Malays. This accentuated the effect of the inevitable concentration of secondary schools in urban areas for economic reasons.

It was necessary to give a university education to as high a proportion as possible of the Malays with secondary education; and a ratio of three Malay scholarships to one non-Malay for most scholarships from public funds has been adopted,[9] notwithstanding the fact that the ratio of candidates of equal ability would be more like one Malay to three non-Malays. This has produced Malays with some university training, and even a number of graduates, to staff the state and federal services. But the standard has not been high, and the superior attractiveness of the

[9] This policy, which was initiated by Malay leaders in the Federation government, is often attributed by Chinese to the University of Malaya, which is wrongly accused of reserving places for Malays. These complaints have been so widespread as to deceive a usually careful American scholar. See F. H. H. King, *The New Malayan Nation: A Study of Communalism and Nationalism* (New York: Institute of Pacific Relations, 1957), pp. 26, 46.

federal service has diverted most of the best talent away from the states. On balance, the effect of this has been to weaken the prestige and effectiveness of state governments. In education the effect of a weak and pro-Malay state government combined with an acute shortage of high-grade Malay teachers has probably been to hamper local educational developments. In land and mining policy it is virtually certain that the delay in encouraging new prospecting and opening up of new areas by road building, drainage, and irrigation has been aggravated by the weakness of state governments.

In addition to the administrative weakness of the state governments, there have been financial obstacles to economic development. Until very recently the revenue of the states was wholly inadequate for the functions which they were required to carry out, and they had to rely on the Federation government for grants, which were given on the basis of their estimates but varied from year to year and could not be carried forward from one year to another, lapsing to the Federal Treasury if not spent. This made any long-term planning virtually impossible.

The effects of this financial policy are most apparent when we consider the relation of capital development to booms and slumps in a country dominated by commodities like tin and rubber. When tin and rubber prices are high, labor is absorbed into both industries because it pays the tin mines to exploit low-grade ore at such times, while the rubber smallholders share the work among more people when the industry advances. The time when labor is available for prospecting and development work is when the prices of the major products are low. But if such development in depressions is to be done, it is necessary both to plan in advance and to carry forward funds. The Federal Constitution has in effect prevented such carry-forward.

The administrative weakness of the states is likely to continue, though improvements in the system of financial allocations were made in 1956[10] when savings were allowed to be carried forward, and further improvements recommended by the Reid Commission, notably some decentralization of tin-mining revenue, have been adopted in the new Constitution. A land development authority has also been appointed as a result of the International Bank Mission's Report. A new impetus has also been given to education by the adoption of the Razak plan for a system of national schools and an expansion of secondary education in the Malay language.

We may inquire, however, whether the new Federal Constitution will not bring another difficulty. From now on the state governments will be not local secretariats but governments operated by political parties. The division of subjects between the Federation and the states, however, is modified only slightly from that which was designed for a Federation unified by a transferable British civil service. There

[10] Huan Tzu Hong, "The New System of Revenue Allocation to the States and Settlements in the Federation of Malaya," *Malayan Economic Review*, II, No. 1 (April, 1957), 79-83.

can be no certainty from now on that we shall avoid
inconsistencies in local taxation and in land development policy, which may interfere with the unity of
Malaya's economy.

These examples suggest that the pattern of *ad hoc*
political development has done notable harm as well
as good to the economic growth of Malaya. In the
main this harm has resulted from neglecting the economic implications of political developments which
have been considered desirable on non-economic
grounds.

Probably the explanation of this neglect is to be
found in relations between the commercial community
and the government community in a comparatively
distant British colony where the influence of the man
on the spot is likely to be unusually strong. Colonial
nationalists often suggest that colonial policy is dominated by trade interests, either because that is
direct policy or because of the social relations between
the commercial and business communities. In practice
the record often shows a scrupulous awareness that
the interests of the peasant or worker are the care of
the government and may differ from those of the
commercial community. It might be truer to suggest
that economic *development* has been identified until
fairly recently with the European business community
and those sections of the local business community
which are most closely associated with it; so that the
process of *ad hoc* political adjustment becomes one
of weighing economic development against other desirable political objectives, rather than working out

the implications for economic development of different political solutions.[11]

A rather different example of the economic consequences of *ad hoc* political solutions is found in the relations between the territories in northern Borneo. Before the Second World War there was no very great need to introduce co-ordination among the Borneo territories. It was possible to regard the different river systems as more or less similar to different islands which were administered according to their needs and had economic relations with the entrepôt center at Singapore. Sarawak continued to be administered by the Brooke family, and its civil service was separate from that of Malaya. Brunei was a sultanate; and it was, therefore, convenient to treat it as an unfederated Malay state along with the other five Malay states which were outside the Federation. Labuan was an entrepôt port and a British colony and was administered as one of the Straits Settlements directly controlled from Singapore. North Borneo was administered by a chartered company.

Development in these territories was carried out by private enterprise with a local center in Singapore and a more distant center in London. Needless to say, such enterprise operated within limits set by the native policy of the Brookes, the monopoly of the chartered company, or the suspicions of the Sultan of Brunei.

After the Second World War the arrangements

[11] Furnivall, *Colonial Policy and Practice*, pp. 280-318; J. H. Boeke, *Economics and Economic Policies of Dual Societies* (Haarlem: H. D. T. Willink, 1953), pp. 79-86, 209-240.

in Malaya precluded the continued existence of Brunei as one of the unfederated states and of Labuan as one of the Straits Settlements. Dynastic and political difficulties led to the cession of Sarawak by the last rajah, and the reconstruction of North Borneo could not be left to a chartered company.

Any tidy-minded non-British administrator would certainly have considered it appropriate to make use of the flexibility introduced by the reconquest of the area and the unquestioned political supremacy of the controlling power to unify all these territories into a single economic unit with properly planned institutions that would guide development in the direction of an ultimate merger into a United East Indies State. The actual policy adopted was one of giving over-all encouragement to united action among the Malayan and Borneo territories by the appointment of a single Governor-General for the whole area (whose office was later merged with that of the Special Commissioner for Southeast Asia). Apart from this, however, local political and economic developments were treated largely independently, with the maximum possible respect for the degree of political independence enjoyed each in its own way by these different political units.

The former relation of Brunei to the Governor of the Straits Settlements (who was also High Commissioner for the Malay States) was transferred to the Governor of Sarawak, who became High Commissioner for Brunei. Labuan was incorporated in North Borneo when the latter became a colony, much as Penang had been incorporated in the Malayan Union. In the immediate postwar years the merchants of Labuan had less success than those of Penang in defending the free-port status of their entrepôt port; but recent events have turned the tables. Labuan has regained its free-port status, while that of Penang is once more under attack.

The powers of the Governor-General's office were very different from those formerly enjoyed by the Governor and High Commissioner in Singapore, whose territory was only slightly smaller since it included Brunei and Labuan in addition to Malaya. The Governor-General's responsibilities were limited to co-ordination and included no administrative or executive functions at all. As a result, no departments were encouraged to develop which would operate throughout the whole area of Malaya and British Borneo, although a number of conferences, for example that of the Directors of Education of all the territories, were arranged from time to time. Prewar economic cohesion and central direction, such as they were, were sacrificed, and the rather loose plans for co-ordination of the whole area probably actually diminished the amount of co-ordination that might have been achieved in northern Borneo. It was only in 1953, when Malayan independence began to appear imminent, that a formal, regular conference of the three Borneo territories was established.

Looking at the British Southeast Asian area from an economic point of view, we could envisage two alternative systems of development. The first is a thorough-going integration of Malaya and British Borneo in which the commercial skill, technical training, and surplus labor of Singapore could help to develop the Borneo territories as a whole, while the oil revenues of Brunei and Sarawak would pay for development not merely in the British Borneo area but in Malaya itself as well. This objective could not have been achieved completely without a major political transformation, but if this economic objective had been kept in mind, the Malay reactions against the McMichael Treaties in Malaya and the Cession Agreement in Sarawak would have been differently handled, and at least some co-ordinating departments for the whole area would have been established so as to give the various separate political units that were emerging a strong focus for Federal thinking.

This large-scale co-ordination may well have been regarded as impracticable, but it is extraordinary that the alternative policy of securing a co-ordination for all three Borneo territories was not pushed through. This would have precluded the present ludicrous situation in which revenue that would have made a material difference in developing the roads, river transport, and education for all Borneo is retained as an unproductive surplus by a local government representing less than one-fifteenth of its total population.

Brunei had just been reconquered from the Japanese, and it would certainly have been possible to enforce a Federation leaving the sultan with powers similar to those of the sultans in the former Fed-

erated Malay States before the decentralization policy. Oil revenue could have been made a central
revenue by levying an export duty rather than a
royalty, if this had seemed more convenient; and as
a result physical equipment could have been built and
institutions developed which would certainly in the
long run have brought more benefit even to Brunei
as a central part, and the wealthiest part, of a prosperous Federation than has accrued by building up
large surpluses in sterling securities.

It can be argued, even with so tiny a state as Brunei, that the controlling power is a trustee, separately,
both for Brunei and for the other territories and must
maintain, in its advice to Brunei, a schizophrenic regard for the interest of Brunei's citizens only and,
therefore, must not use Brunei's revenue for wider
development purposes. If this logical position is
maintained, it seems wholly unreasonable to establish
a High Commissioner for Brunei in Sarawak and
allow him to enforce uniform salary conditions which
prevent Brunei from attracting the cream of Sarawak's economy and in other ways to co-ordinate
policy in all respects other than that of transferring
revenue.

If there had been a genuine sensitiveness to the
separateness of the interests of Brunei and Sarawak,
it would have been possible to allow Brunei to spend
its revenues independently and give the Resident of
Brunei full powers to develop his state at the expense
of the economies of the neighboring countries. This
would have introduced much more rapid develop-

ment in Brunei at the expense of less rapid development in the neighboring territories.

There was clearly no such genuine sensitiveness to the separateness of the interests of the different states. This was simply another instance of an *ad hoc* political adjustment in which it was felt necessary to avoid conflicts with the sultan through whom control was exercised, even though this meant deferring development of the whole area for a generation. The *ad hoc* political solution was to appoint a resident to advise the sultan and thereby to establish a vested interest in the existing revenues accruing to the state. This vested interest was strong enough to protect itself on such matters as the collection and distribution of revenue but not on salaries or even on land-tenure or development policy.

We here encounter one of the curiosities of the British system of colonial development which has often led to our being considered hypocritical in our attitude to development. We have been accused of a policy of divide and rule in most of the territories in which we have exercised control, and we almost invariably leave behind difficult problems of integration, such as the Hindu-Muslim problem in India, because of this basic attitude. I refer to our basic attitude of separate obligation to almost any group which feels itself to be different, provided its interest does not conflict too strongly with the basic purpose for which power was secured in the first instance.[12]

[12] Lord Hailey's *African Survey: Revised 1956* (New York: Oxford University Press, 1957) deals extensively with similar problems in another region.

SOUTHEAST ASIA

To discuss this fully it is necessary to devote a little attention to the basic characteristics of political power in relation to the colonization process. Wherever people are governed without formal institutions for eliciting their consent, there is, from the point of view of a democrat, some violation of democratic principles. It appears to be believed in the United States that if the skin color or language or certain other characteristics of the ruler differ from those of the ruled, this violation of democratic principles is necessarily aggravated.

The logic of this position has always escaped me, particularly when the difference between the ruler and the ruled is such that the ruler tends to be submitted to certain democratic pressures from elsewhere which the ruled could not exercise for lack of any experience of democracy. I should argue that wherever a resident or adviser from a democratic country is substituted for an absolute monarch, there is some gain in democratic control even though there may be other disadvantages to the country concerned. Democracy is a thing that can to some extent be transmitted like other features of the culture of a ruling group.

In the British Commonwealth, however, it is not part of the pattern to try to incorporate the local population by cultural change into a large supernational empire but rather to introduce piecemeal a number of British institutions, modified to local circumstances as they seem necessary, with the ultimate objective of building up a separate state which will have permanently absorbed along with its own local characteristics certain British institutions.

This makes it a matter of some importance to decide what is the unit through which rule will be exercised. This, however, is rarely decided on any principle but is a matter of political tact following the line of least resistance. If it is convenient and will cause minimum political strife to govern through an existing sultan, even if his territory is hopelessly inadequate for a modern state, he will become the unit through which rule is exercised and his advisers, although they are British, will become a vested interest and will preserve the sultan's position against the requirements of any wider unit to the limit of their powers. Moreover, this does not apply only to territorial units. The Chinese of the Straits Settlements were administered through their own community leaders, and this policy, which fostered a system of bidding for leadership within the community, has helped to perpetuate the communal pattern in modern Malaya.[13]

Where necessary, the interests of separate groups will be co-ordinated subsequently by some form of negotiation or by administrative action. But the criterion of what is necessary does not include maximum economic development as a necessity, except where there is some organized industry to exert pressure; and even then, as in the Federated Malay States, the

[13] V. W. W. Purcell, *The Chinese in Malaya* (London: Oxford University Press, 1948), and, by contrast, G. W. Skinner, "Chinese Assimilation and Thai Politics," *Journal of Asian Studies*, XVI (1957), 237-250.

pressure may be resisted on political grounds. Some of the ordinary unifying forces of political and economic life, which would tend to operate if the aim was simply to reproduce a political and economic society on Western lines, are inhibited by the felt need to look after many conflicting interests which have established themselves as political influences within the British system.

The exercise of any political power involves by its very nature the subordination of the interests of particular individuals or groups within an area to what is regarded as the interest of the area as a whole. It is possible, however, to proceed much further by agreement if separate groups are treated separately and if each is given what is acceptable to it, while compromises are worked out on the political plane with reference to the basic purposes for which it was necessary to secure power. But almost by definition, a territory under colonial rule is incapable itself of providing a defensible and viable political unit. It is something of a paradox that both for political and for economic development it is necessary to exercise more power than would be needed simply to keep the different parts of the territory in harmony with one another. The exercise of the minimum power which is consistent with basic objectives will be a policy that hampers economic (as well as political) development, if economic development is not one of those basic objectives.

In the region of northern Borneo, the oil interests were able to press for facilities to develop the oil industry itself, but there was no material advantage to them in joint arrangements between Brunei and Sarawak. The oil is actually physically exported from Sarawak territory, and the division of the government revenues between royalty, export duty, and income tax is largely a matter of negotiation. So long as a Federation was not brought into being, any diversion of Brunei's revenue to other needs could be forcibly represented by the Resident of Brunei as a robbery of this state, but if a federal structure had been imposed, this would have no more weight than an objection by Trengganu that an export duty on iron ore was used not for the benefit of Trengganu but for the whole of the Federation of Malaya.

The point that needs to be made is that where the central power exists and can control such things as conditions of service for government servants, relations with outside bodies, etc., it cannot really avoid the responsibility of either harmonizing or refusing to harmonize the conflicting interests of different groups. It is not really possible to be a trustee simultaneously for different and conflicting interests. The British system makes us often attempt this impossible task, but there is no consistency in the matters in which local interests are protected. Broadly speaking, efforts at co-ordination are made only when they are politically necessary for the continued existence of the co-ordinating power or when the conflict of interests interferes with important objects of policy.

It is probably fair to say that in the Borneo territories in postwar years the long-run interest of government has been concentrated on preventing irreconcilable conflicts between the different British territories of Borneo and Malaya so as to leave the way open to a possible political union later, and this has meant that there is no very active interest in treating the three Borneo territories as a whole. It is only in the last few months, since the achievement of independence by Malaya, that the governors of Sarawak and North Borneo have reopened the issue of a federation of the three territories. But it has been made clear that the federation envisaged is one in which Brunei's revenue would remain separate, and not be merged in federal revenue, even if some of it might be used for development in the form of loans.

I turn next to consider some of the consequences of the freedom allowed to the men on the spot in the development toward self-government of British colonial territories. This has had many favorable consequences for economic development by giving scope for local political enterprise as well as economic enterprise. The development of trade in Penang in its early days by Francis Light, the foundation of Singapore by Stamford Raffles, the building up of the state of Sarawak under the rule of three successive rajahs of the Brooke family, and the growth of the various chartered companies are all examples where economic development has been possible because individuals or small groups on the spot saw opportunities for development and were able to take advantage of them. The support given to these men has often been grudging, and in reading about nineteenth-century development, one is frequently impressed with the caution and reluctance of London. Yet the degree of autonomy given to the men on the spot is an underlying feature of the whole development. This is only in part a matter of deliberate policy. It arises partly from the great distances over which control was exercised and the willingness of large sections of the British middle class to seek careers which kept them away from their homes for most of their working lives.

Clearly the use of British power to back up the work of the creative administrator on the spot has led to greater enterprise and more information about the territories than would have been found with a more centralized government. I am here, however, concerned with certain other aspects of the system which are rather less favorable. Where the interests of the man on the spot do not favor economic development, the system often works less satisfactorily for economic development than a more centralized system. Examples can be given from the development of smallholders' rubber, the measures to encourage local manufacturing in Malaya, and the design of training for development, including both the structure of institutions and the process of education itself.

It has already been indicated that the development of rubber smallholdings has not enjoyed a great deal of government support. In the early days, before the First World War, the rubber boom was regarded as something temporary and uncertain, and the desertion by Malays of their traditional rice growing was viewed with some alarm. The rice shortages which followed the First World War had an altogether disproportionate effect in encouraging this attitude, so that for nearly twenty years there was a tendency to discourage the drift away from padi as a means of aiming at self-sufficiency in food. But the most striking example was the underassessment of smallholdings during the two rubber-regulation schemes, greatly restricting the tendency which otherwise would doubtless occur for the smallholdings to replace the estates in the natural rubber industry.[14]

It will be noted that at no stage was the opposition to rubber smallholdings directly related to a desire to leave a clear field for European-owned rubber estates. I should personally estimate that the paternal influence of the Malay sultans, anxious over the decline of old customs, would have had as much effect on policy during the first rubber boom as any influence of the new planters.

The desire to achieve self-sufficiency in food, though economically misguided, certainly seems to have been genuine, though it was not strong enough to stand in the way of the development of the estate rubber industry. The underassessment of smallholders was a result partly of lack of information

[14] P. T. Bauer, *The Rubber Industry: A Study of Competition and Monopoly* (Cambridge, Mass.: Harvard University Press, 1948); Bauer, *Report on a Visit to Rubber Growing Smallholdings in Malaya.*

about the characteristics of smallholding rubber and partly of the employment as assessors of unemployed planters who tended to judge smallholdings by criteria appropriate only to estates. Poor standards of maintenance or poor economy of labor on an estate would be a reasonable indication of low yields; and in the absence of other information, we need not assume any unreasonable bias against the smallholders when they were underassessed. The absence of information, however, was partly due to the social and political climate that was unfavorable to economic development in this sphere and partly to the deliberate exclusion by the estate rubber producers of economic aspects of the industry from the research program of the Rubber Research Institute.[15]

An obvious line of economic development for Singapore is the growth of industrialization through extending the activities of small capitalists, principally Chinese, for whom a most flexible system exists by which an enterprising man can acquire capital and connections, starting from very small beginnings. In its recent *Report* on economic development in Malaya, the International Bank has emphasized the importance of this kind of industry and the desirability of enabling individual firms to grow to a rather larger size. It is rather striking that in all the studies made by Chinese-speaking administrative officers of the Singapore government and the former governments of the Straits Settlements and

[15] P. T. Bauer, "The Working of Rubber Regulation," *Economic Journal*, LIV (1946) 391-414.

the Federated Malay States, virtually no attention has been paid to the methods of organizing trade credit or to techniques of capital formation among the Chinese merchants of Southeast Asia. In the framework of a Chinese partnership, the European legal concepts of either unlimited liability or formal limited liability structure seem highly inappropriate; the systems of trade credit are little understood and frequently subject to official criticism as tending to restrict competition; while the tontine system, which is an important source of long-term capital, is given no legal sanction. My own knowledge of Chinese is, I fear, negligible, so that I cannot discuss these business techniques with any authority; but it would appear that if economic development as such had been an active concern of governments in the past, greater attempts would have been made to devise a framework that would integrate these techniques within a system of the rule of law and objective recording.

Finally, we turn to the complex question of training for economic development. I am not here referring to the training of artisans, which is a special and highly difficult problem in Malaya, largely unrelated to the Commonwealth theme. Even commercial education is only a small part of the training in question. I am referring to the attitude of the local business and government community to the training of the local population through the appropriate design of institutions. Here the attitudes themselves are complex, and I can claim only to be giving personal impressions from some twenty years of experience during a time of radical change in both attitudes and political background.

I should on the whole criticize the British system as tending to lead to too limited a range and volume of this class of education because of the hostility of the local European population to any widespread expansion. I should not, however, wish to be misunderstood and certainly would not suggest that this opposition was normally deliberate and consciously designed to maintain the European monopoly.

Probably the most important difference between British and, say, American attitudes in this respect is the much greater emphasis on character and cultural characteristics (using the word "culture" in the anthropological sense) within the British system. It is very strongly believed that fitness for responsibility in a modern business or a modern state depends much more on certain developments of character (or changes in outlook) than on technical knowledge. This is partly the result of the existence of a more or less permanently domiciled European community. Such a community becomes more aware of the significance of cultural differences, but it may also tend to use them as a protective mechanism.

A Chinese clerk, storeman, or salesman plays a certain role in a European organization. His attitude to his role and hence his performance of it will depend on his general cultural background. It is not characteristic of a British domiciled community to believe that if a Chinese is taught enough English he will behave as an Englishman when put in the appropriate setting. This is a sensible attitude and much nearer to the facts than the naïve belief that racial discrimination is involved when appointment to a post is treated differently according to the race of the person concerned. It is a waste of manpower, which no economist should view with equanimity, to try to design jobs in such a way that they could be done equally well by an Englishman or a Chinese in a Kuala Lumpur setting. If one did design a job in this way, it would mean, for example, building up wholly unnecessary safeguards for the Englishman against the subtle pressure of entertainment, clan spirit, etc., which tends to undermine a Chinese in such a position, while providing unnecessary machinery for contacts and interpreting to the Chinese.

Because this attempt to treat the jobs as different is accompanied by discrimination against the educated Asian in salary, etc., the pressure from the Asian side is towards uniformity of paper qualifications and attacks on discrimination. This in turn leads to a reaction of discounting paper qualifications and tending to run down the abilities of the Asian intellectual. The root cause of the trouble seems to be the view that you should first aim at educating the Asian to be as good a substitute for the European as possible in character and outlook, and then recognize that this cannot be done completely and give him a lower-grade job, rather like the European's, in which he will be treated as a rather imperfect substitute.

The development problem is one of finding suitable modes of training to develop modern business and political institutions in an Asian cultural setting. The domiciled European community in the British system is not consciously trying to carry out any such policy laid down in the United Kingdom but is merely reproducing the best approximations it can to British institutions in a colonial setting, redesigned to use Asians in subordinate positions. Adaptation to existing factor scarcities is quite good, but what is needed is design for growth.

The absence of any such design has led to our present situation in which we are hurriedly trying to make up for what is alleged to be neglect in training large numbers of Asian substitutes for Europeans in all kinds of jobs designed for Europeans, many of them much less appropriate to the local situation than would have been the jobs created for a local population with local knowledge and local needs.

These educational phenomena all tend to confirm Asian nationalists in the belief that the progress of colonies towards self-government is not something which the British government genuinely desires but is a mere piece of propaganda belied by the facts of training. My own view is a little more lenient to my own countrymen. I feel that there has been a genuine intention to increase local training as well as economic development but that the pattern of political improvisation and the excessive influence of a local European community with long-term residence in the country has tended to generate institutions not really suited to either political or economic development.

With the achievement of self-government, the immediate effect will no doubt be an expansion in the existing education system and the training of large numbers of local people to do jobs formerly done by Europeans. It may be some time before it is fully realized how different the plans for political and economic development should be for a self-governing country from those which are appropriate to a colony run by foreigners.

This is a point that needs great emphasis. An already harmful situation has been gravely aggravated by the facile generalizations of the Atlantic Charter and by emphasis on an absence of racial discrimination. I am not arguing in favor of racial discrimination but of the use of intelligence both to forecast what kind of cultural changes will be necessary or desirable and to adapt employment opportunities and training so that unnecessary and irrelevant cultural changes need not be enforced. This implies that the character both of the state and of the economy will be modified as local people become available in place of foreigners. I feel that this is the respect in which the evolutionary *ad hoc* pattern of development within the Commonwealth has shown itself least satisfactory and that it would only be a logical line of advance if the goal envisaged was that the entire culture should be transformed to model itself on the British pattern.

To some extent Macaulay had this in mind, at

least in the political and economic sphere, in India: a fantastic vision but one that made better sense than the present pattern of training up Asian successors for the holders of European posts in a colonial environment. There would be some point in trying to train up the kind of civil servants and teachers that would be needed if Malaya were to become a replica of Britain. But the civil servants and teachers of colonial Malaya could not possibly be even plausible imitations of their counterparts in England so long as they occupied the role they did in Malaya. Yet, somehow, the combination of the Commonwealth structure with postwar ideas of non-discrimination has led to serious attempts being made to train up Malayans to take over the British colonial structure.

This applies not only in government but even in businesses, so that instead of thinking out what is the best way in which British training could help the growth of Chinese business, we are trying to train Chinese to fill the posts in a system based on the concentration of managerial skills and responsibilities in European hands. Chinese are very adaptable people, but it is not unnatural that they find this role rather difficult to fill and that European employers complain that their subordinates cannot learn to treat these men as Europeans.

I am not certain that anything better than this could be done; possibly the redesigning of training methods to fit the local cultural environment is something that must be done with a sharp reaction after independence is achieved. I believe that the standard of education given in the British system is reasonably high but that it is ill directed and insufficient in quantity, imposing a very heavy strain at the time when independence is achieved.

The problem of promoting economic development is largely one of stimulating and guiding cultural change in the direction of those activities which in the long run will raise the people's standard of living. It is doubtful that it is even theoretically possible for a group of people to design an educational system for the promotion of a given cultural change. Any such design would imply an ability in the educators to step outside their own culture, which we can hardly postulate. We can only inquire in what respects the system of rule is favorable to the kind of cultural change that development seems to demand.

We must realize first of all that although people may want economic development, they may not want all cultural changes to be subordinated to this one aim. The adaptation would normally come about partly by imitation, partly by proselytizing, and partly by commercial enterprise. I would argue that the structure of the British system, with large numbers of Englishmen resident for long enough to form a settled class but not intermarrying with the population, tends to create a special colonial culture enjoying great local prestige but not really adapted to rapid economic development except of that sector of the economy which is directly related to government or export trade. Chinese business has no doubt flourished in Southeast Asia under British rule, but the cultural setting has not been helpful toward solving the problems of economic growth for this important sector of the economy, nor has it helped to integrate it with the remainder.

It would be foolish to suggest that British colonial society has merely tended to reproduce overseas an exact replica of British life. It has shown plenty of inventiveness and capacity to adapt itself to the circumstances, but the important question is whether it has generated institutions which will be useful after the Europeans leave. There is a sharp difference between those territories in which the Europeans have become demographically dominant as in Australia, New Zealand, and Canada; those in which they have become settled and politically dominant but remained demographically unimportant as in East Africa, South Africa, and perhaps the West Indies; and those in which they have not settled at all but have exercised control through long-term but not permanent residents as in Asia, West Africa, and the Pacific territories.

The first group has adapted British institutions to local needs in a way which is appropriate to long-run development. Australia and New Zealand have very different social structures from England but their culture is appropriate to their own problems. In the East and South African territories a local white culture develops which is intensely conscious that its survival depends not on assimilation of the local population but on preserving its separateness. I find it difficult to see any solution within a purely

local setting for the economic development of the
bulk of the population of these territories. The
problem is difficult and intractable. It might be
solved under a dictatorship which was confident of
retaining power over both races alike, however much
the more backward race developed. Similarly, it
might be solved within the framework of a wider
federation in which the local minority's fears could
be allayed by bringing in a majority which was culturally allied to them but at the same time interested
in a cultural transformation of the remainder for the
sake of economic development. But neither of these
solutions is relevant to our Commonwealth problems.

It is the third type of territory that chiefly interests us here, where a transient group of Europeans
builds up a culture for themselves which the local
population at first wishes to imitate but which is not
appropriate to the local setting once the Europeans
leave.

We may illustrate by considering a few of the
institutional inventions that have affected the economy in Southeast Asia but are not obviously appropriate to a purely local economy where Europeans
have ceased to exercise the control. We may consider first the stabilization devices which have helped
the economies to withstand the enormous fluctuations
in prosperity that arise from the instability of primary
product prices. Then we can turn to the organization of trade credit, the system of commercial education, and the structure of the agency house system.

Four different stabilization techniques have grown up within the colonial setting and have enabled the Southeast Asian economies to withstand, without unduly serious consequences, fluctuations in national income on a quite horrifying scale. First, there are the fiscal devices which have tended to build up substantial surpluses when the national income was large and deficits when it was small. The graduated export duty, in which the rate of *ad valorem* tax depends on the price of the commodity, rising steeply at high prices, was probably rather a happy accident than a piece of successful economic planning.[16] The course of events seems to have been that a graduated export duty of this kind was first imposed on tin in Malaya, varying with the price because export duty was regarded as a convenient substitute for a royalty. Later, the Sarawak government adapted this duty structure to rubber and certain other products with a view to expanding revenue when the new colonial status of the territory made an expansion in revenue necessary. It was this graduated export duty which was taken as a precedent in the Federation of Malaya as a deliberate anti-inflationary device in the early stages of the Korean War boom. These graduated export duties are extremely rapid and effective stabilizers and will probably continue to be used so long as the economies remain dependent on unstable export products.

On the expenditure side there has been automatic stabilization as a result of the fact that ambitious

[16] Silcock, *Fiscal Survey.*

schemes can be pushed by colonial governments through a generally unsympathetic local finance committee in boom times but cannot be carried through then for lack of labor. Commitments are generally entered into which prevent the expenditures being canceled during less prosperous times, so that the expenditure pattern reinforces the variation in revenue by causing corrective surpluses and deficits. This latter piece of stabilization technique is one which will be less appropriate in an independent government, where the finance committee has ceased to be in effect an opposition body with limited power. Indeed, the whole organization of colonial public finance, although it works fairly satisfactorily within the colonial setting, is very bad training for financial responsibility and perhaps particularly for fiscal techniques of stabilization.

In an economy such as that of Malaya, stabilization will involve budgeting for both surpluses and deficits. This is difficult in a democracy, which needs a great deal of education before it can tackle inflation by fiscal measures. A background of a break with colonial rule might conceivably be useful in encouraging the right policy if it occurred during a depression, but the lesson would probably do lasting harm by encouraging financial laxity in all circumstances.

The experts are lacking, and even when they exist they lack authority, since they are necessarily Western-educated. Probably the best they could do would be to follow more or less the colonial techniques of stabilization. But they can acquire the authority to do this only if they can produce important innovations in other spheres, such as the development of a capital market.

We turn next to monetary techniques of stabilization. Here the colonial currency system has created a situation in which the colonial territories are virtually an extension of the British monetary system, so that there is an automatic tendency for surpluses to be built up and held outside the colony in boom times and to be repatriated to meet expenses during depressions. So far as this goes, it has some stabilizing effect on colonial economies and diminishes the worst effects of unstable primary product prices. It does little to encourage capital formation during depressions when local factors of production are available, but does help to prevent some of the effects of excessive demand for labor during a boom.

Here again the system is by no means a mere adaptation of the British economy and is fairly well suited to the colonial situation. It is not, however, a very satisfactory stepping stone toward the kind of financial structure that will be relevant to the development of an independent country.

In this connection it is probably worthwhile to comment that the entrepôt ports might be best served even after independence by retaining something very like a colonial currency system. This is indeed one of the sources of potential conflict between the Federation of Malaya and Singapore, since the Central Bank structure recommended in the local Watson-

Caine Report on the Central Bank seemed more suitable to Singapore's requirements than to those of the Federation and may generate a dangerous tendency to separation in currency matters between the two territories.

Fiscal and financial stabilization schemes have been supplemented by direct controls of two kinds: the international control schemes for rubber and tin and the control of inward and outward migration. It goes without saying that independent countries will need new techniques if they are to participate in international control schemes, but these will simply be the techniques of participating in international life which Commonwealth countries are normally enabled to learn gradually as their independence of action grows. I believe this is one of the greatest advantages that colonial territories in the British system derive from the Commonwealth structure, though it is one which is not often mentioned. I do not wish to comment on it further in this chapter.

The fourth method of stabilization was adjustment of the labor force by control of migration. This was carried out very systematically with Indian labor, recruited mainly for European estates and for the Public Works Department. Wages in certain key areas were deliberately pegged at a level determined by a standard laborer's budget, which represented a level of living considered appropriate by the Labor Department. This level was a good deal higher than the same men would have enjoyed in India, but it represented a conscious effort to supply cheap labor rather than an attempt to recruit immigrants and potential citizens. Migration, inwards and outwards, was deliberately controlled to maintain these income levels.

With Chinese labor, there was a similar control over inward movements only. The government did not organize immigration of Chinese itself but adjusted the numbers of male immigrants by regulation, leaving it to the shipping companies to arrange the selection. There was no deliberate regulation to maintain a standard wage, but the numbers of male immigrants allowed varied with the state of employment.

Since the war there has been very little immigration, for political reasons. The Malays are anxious about political control and do not want more non-Malay immigrants. On purely economic grounds selective immigration could still be useful in Malaya, and even unselective immigration might help Brunei and North Borneo. And if there were a general inward flow, some stabilization might be achieved by controlling its volume.

It is unlikely, however, that as independence comes to these areas, they will wish to face the problems of new immigration. Probably the availability of this stabilizer in the past has hampered the development of other stabilizers, and migration itself will no longer be able to fulfil this role.

We have seen that of the four stabilizers, the fiscal and monetary ones might still be appropriate, but neither the political nor the technical conditions for their use have been created; more complex methods are likely to be attempted but will encounter great difficulties. International control schemes offer more hope if agreement can be reached through Commonwealth machinery, while migration has ceased to be a practical stabilizer.

We turn next to the organization of credit. Here the colonial pattern is broadly one in which short-term capital from the London money market (including, of course, short-term capital from Malaya held in London and used as part of the resources of the London money market) finds its way to local businesses through two channels. Partly, the exchange banks have their own systems of *compradores* and local information through which they can lend directly to the more reliable Chinese firms; and, partly, the credit is mediated through the large European firms which get short-term credit for quite considerable periods from the banks and are able thereby to give credit to Chinese and Indian wholesalers and dealers. Some of the Chinese firms in turn, if they can make rapid sales of goods supplied by European firms, can make use of their trade credit to finance other business for which direct credit would have been either very costly or unobtainable.

It might have seemed more desirable to use the great fund of commercial skill that exists in Singapore to build up a local short-term money market with forms of financial instruments that corresponded to the needs of local business. This has not been done, but the situation in this respect is much more favorable than in some others. A considerable system of local banks exists, which at present is partly an intermediary between the European banks and the public—mainly the Chinese traders—but which has developed techniques of financing business reasonably well adapted to local trading conditions.

It should be a fairly simple matter when the Central Bank is established to build up a local money market between the Central Bank, the local banks, and the foreign exchange banks. The difficulty will be the modification of the banking system's relations with London. For the Central Bank to exercise a reasonable degree of control and to stimulate a local money market it will be necessary for the bank to be able to insist on local banks holding their reserves with it. At the same time, it would be undesirable to contract unduly the contacts with London of the Imperial banks which at present play a leading part in local banking.

Something will need to be arranged which comes midway between retaining the existing system in which the Malayan currency and credit structure is simply an extension of the London money market and, on the other hand, treating the Imperial banks as purely foreign banks doing exchange business and occupying a peripheral place in the country's money market. The precise position which these banks occupy will depend on the relative weight given to the Federation's point of view and to that of Singapore. For maximum control and also for the national independence of Malaya it would be desirable to force these Imperial banks to become something much more like a local bank under the control of the Central Bank in policy matters, or else to compel them to limit their operations in the internal trade of the country. On the other hand, Singapore's position within Southeast Asia is fairly closely linked with its contacts with the London money market, and Central Bank policies which interfered too much with this contact would undermine Singapore's trading position.

There are, however, a number of cross-currents. Singapore's politics are rather more left-wing than those of the Federation, and in the long run this may tend to operate against the pre-eminence of the mercantile interests in Malayan banking. Moreover, the Federation, while desiring to strengthen its Central Bank, would probably prefer to retain the Imperial banks with a modified relation to the Central Bank if the alternative was to strengthen the financial power of Chinese banks and hence of Chinese business within the economy of the Federation. At present the only local banks in sight are Chinese banks, though a beginning of Malay banking can be detected in the co-operative movement.

Whatever compromise is reached, a local money market will need to be built up, and one of the chief problems in creating it will be the changes that need to be introduced into the organization of credit adapted to local British business.

Finally, something needs to be said about the agency house system and the kind of modifications that will need to be made in its structure after independence. The term "agency house" is a rather loose one and covers not only the great trading companies which are agents for large numbers of manufacturers all over the world, normally on an exclusive agency basis, but also the shipping agents who engage in a good deal of local shipping and other business and the secretarial companies which manage the affairs of many plantations and mines, often without owning a controlling interest.

The main role of these agency houses is to provide a link in which the overseas trader or investor will have confidence, partly because it is European-owned and controlled and partly because it has the accounting skills and general financial techniques which are so much scarcer than enterprise in the Malayan economy. It is clearly a problem of some importance to determine how these businesses, which at present occupy so important a position in the Malayan economy, can adapt their functions to fit in with an independent country.

Clearly, the maintenance of European control as a basis for generating overseas confidence is unlikely to be tolerated indefinitely. As in any independent country, there will be in Malaya attempts to bring the economy of the country under the control of its own nationals. At present, however, the agency houses appear merely to envisage the training of increasing numbers of local people to occupy the junior administrative positions within a largely unchanged organization. It would appear probable that this will be an unsatisfactory compromise since it will turn the businesses into organizations that are neither wholly under European control nor acceptable to the local government. In the long run, if these businesses are to continue to contribute effectively to the Malayan economy, it would appear to be necessary for them either to turn over more and more of their lines of business to local control while retaining their financial interest, or, alternatively, to assume the function of a managing and financial corporation which will increasingly train up its own local staff to undertake new development work for local business.[17]

For the latter type of organization there is very great need in most newly independent countries, and this is a function which the agency houses could continue to fulfil while adapting themselves to an independent country. It is to be hoped that development will in fact take this direction rather than the other, since it would be unfortunate if the growth of centralized planning that is bound to occur in some sectors of the economy should lead to the loss of the special financial and managerial skills that European private enterprise has introduced.

In this sphere as in government and in financial undertakings the institutions that have developed

[17] It is necessary to emphasize that it will not be possible for them to play this role unless a proper capital market can also be developed in which capital gains can be taken by selling shares to local shareholders as subsidiary businesses become established.

have been strongly influenced by the needs of a resident British community, and the coming of independence will involve strains on the capacity for improvisation of both the local population and the Europeans themselves.

3

Assessment and Suggestions

In this chapter I propose to make an assessment of the economic position and prospects for the British territories in Southeast Asia, and to indicate possible action by the remainder of the Commonwealth and by Americans interested in the Commonwealth. I shall begin by discussing the development needs of the region, go on to consider Commonwealth economic relations to these territories, and finish by discussing what I think friends of the Commonwealth in the United States might be able to do.

The basic development needs of the region can be grouped under seven different headings. First, the basic political requirements; second, the provision and improvement of transport; third, the needs of agriculture and the fishing industry; fourth, industrialization; fifth, currency and credit developments; sixth, the cultural changes implied in economic growth; and finally, the impact of research and outside assistance.

If the region is to develop rapidly, it will need

the maintenance of order, increasing integration of its plural societies, and active leadership in all the changes which development will involve.

In Malaya the politicians start with a tradition of compromise and negotiation which should be useful in maintaining order and encouraging the separate racial and political groups to come together into nations. In the Federation of Malaya there is unfortunately no united national party, but the Alliance shows signs of developing into one.[1] Leadership which is not communal can be provided by the business community and the Malay aristocracy so long as they act together and can secure the support of at least part of the English educated class, including some of the intellectuals of the country. It seems doubtful, however, whether a united, non-communal opposition will arise, and there is some doubt whether this would be desirable. It must not be assumed that parliamentary democracy in any Asian country will necessarily take the form of an alternation of government and opposition, and it might well be more to Malaya's interest if the country were led by a united alliance with opposition from various communal groups, which would help to compel the alliance itself to continue to work by compromise and avoid antagonizing too large a section of any one community. Most Asian nations seem to expect a government that will lead them in a process of rapid change to

[1] The Alliance is now registered as a political party, though membership is still through the constituent parties, the United Malays' National Organization, the Malayan Chinese Association, and the Malayan Indian Congress.

new ways of life and higher economic standards, and it may well be that a government by compromise will be the best solution in Malaya. This may not be helped by the emergence of several alternative kinds of compromise.

As a small country Malaya cannot hope for self-sufficiency, and it is fortunate that its leaders are not particularly concerned to make it self-sufficient. In the past, however, the movement of both capital and labor into Malaya has not been directed with a view to raising the standard of living of the existing population. Malaya's politicians do not seem averse to an inward flow of foreign capital, provided it can be partially controlled so as to raise local standards of living.[2]

It is almost equally important to consider the role of the civil service and its adequacy as an instrument of economic development. The pattern of a specialized civil service carrying out the role of administration under the orders of a political head is something quite unfamiliar to the people of Malaya. They are accustomed, whether under colonial rule or under sultans or other Asian rule, to a more or less political civil service which makes policy as well as conducting administration. The task of the existing civil service is made particularly difficult by the fact that its members have to familiarize the public and the politicians themselves with the role that the civil service is to

[2] See the proposed charter for foreign capital put forward by the Prime Minister, Tunku Abdul Rahman, at the 1958 meeting of the United Nations Economic Commission for Asia and the Far East at Kuala Lumpur, March, 1958.

play. To accept policy decisions from politicians but to refuse to serve either their personal or their individual political ends will be very difficult in a situation in which the public will have no understanding of these distinctions and can easily be led to believe that individual or collective resistance to any politician's wishes means a struggle of the civil service as one source of power against another. The civil service is well organized in trade unions and has been fairly active politically during the later stages of colonial rule. It is most important that the influence which it should have over events in the future shall be the influence of detailed knowledge and exploration of the consequences of policy, and that it shall not become too much of a separate power in the state. There are dangers here, not only because the politicians and the public will find the position hard to understand but because the civil servants themselves have too little experience of responsibility and will be heavily overstrained because of an increasing burden on government and a loss of a high proportion of the experienced European civil servants. The hopeful features are the establishment of civil service commissions to control recruitment and promotion—commissions which have strong popular support—and the considerable amount of training available through international organizations and in the departments of the British civil service. One of the chief difficulties is the fact that the load on the civil service makes it impossible to take advantage of anything like enough of these opportunities.

In Malaya the difficulties have arisen from a comparatively sudden need to transfer power to a civil service organized to fit a small group of Europeans at the top and a subordinate local staff. Replacing the Europeans has proved exceptionally difficult in these conditions. We may inquire how far the three territories in Borneo are being consciously prepared for self-government by anticipating these difficulties.

Perhaps the most hopeful feature here is the strong emphasis on local government and the attempt to use it as an instrument in integrating the different races, to hand increasing numbers of functions over to these local authorities and make them a basis of the power of the central government. There has been, however, far too little allocation of revenue to these local authorities, which have no readily available sources of income adequate for the tasks in providing education, transport, and the like. Partly as a result of the failure to treat the three territories as a single unit, the overhead expenses of central government have used up too high a proportion of the revenues, so that the concept of development through local authorities has not in fact led to a very high rate of local development. The emphasis certainly seems sound, but it is difficult to see how with the existing government structure the local authorities can be given sufficient weight.

Turning next to the provision of transport, the past record in both the present Federation of Malaya and the entrepôt ports has been much more creditable than that in the Borneo territories. The road system, not only in the ports of Singapore and Penang, but throughout Malaya, is of a very high standard. The railways, though less good than the roads in a comparison with the rest of Asia, still reach a high standard of efficiency and of ton-miles per head of the population.[3] Probably these high standards have been due to the availability of tin revenue, but there can be little doubt that the governments of Malaya have throughout their history shown an active awareness of the importance of transport. The chief critical comment which was made by the International Bank Mission in its recent report was an emphasis on the building of feeder roads to open up the rural areas, rather than concentrating on further improvements to the trunk road system.[4]

This comment might have been made more appropriately on transport development in the Borneo territories, but it applies in some measure in all the British territories in the region. The local populations have shown themselves well aware of the advantages of transport, and bicycles are common even in comparatively remote villages, provided there is some kind of track which can reach a road. Truck transport also develops very rapidly even on poor roads when they are first opened up, and this is one of the great difficulties of development in this rain forest country, for as soon as roads begin to be used by

[3] United Nations Economic Commission for Asia and the Far East, *Annual Survey, 1956*, p. 182.

[4] International Bank for Reconstruction and Development, *Economic Development of Malaya* (Baltimore: Johns Hopkins Press, 1955), pp. 80, 290-292.

truck traffic the cost of maintenance on any but the highest quality roads becomes excessive. Consequently the Public Works Departments tend to resist the building of minor roads with an inferior standard of construction.

In spite of these difficulties there can be little doubt that the construction of bicycle tracks usable by light transport, and of earth roads which can be used by trucks in dry weather, greatly increases agricultural productivity. Development takes place when the barge or the outboard motor brings new stretches of river within reach of an ocean port, and when the bicycle or the truck struggling over an earth road brings remoter areas within reach of the river. Two comments need to be made on transport development prospects for the future. The first is that because of the inadequacy of statistics of agriculture in underdeveloped countries, most such countries underestimate the importance of transport in their development work.[5] The second is that the pushing through of a new road greatly increases the relative advantage of those who understand market structure, so that it is desirable to co-ordinate community development and rural extension work with transport development. Unless this is done the local population will be left hopelessly at a disadvantage when the road first arrives.

The neglect of transport as an instrument of de-

[5] P. T. Bauer and B. S. Yamey, *The Economics of Underdeveloped Countries* (Cambridge: Cambridge University Press, 1957), pp. 48-51.

velopment is often accompanied by a tendency to overlook the growth of farms and agricultural equipment in estimating the capital formation that is taking place.[6] Particularly in countries with empty land and increasing populations, one of the most important forms of capital formation is the settlement of new land and the establishment of new fishing communities with their boats and tackle. The great importance of transport is largely due to the fact that the comparative rates of growth of population and of cultivated area are among the most critical factors which determine whether a country like Malaya or Borneo is improving or deteriorating in its level of development.

In Malaya the obstacles to rapid development are political and constitutional rather than strictly economic. It is not that the Malayan state governments are hostile to economic development, but that their administrations tend to lack vigor, and that the necessary research surveys and training would normally be beyond the resources of the individual states. For this reason in the new Constitution, although land development will be the responsibility of the states, provision has been made for Federal authority in research surveys and training.[7] Moreover, the agricultural officers in the different states must accept technical advice from their Federal heads in the Department of Agriculture. The setting up of a Federal

[6] Bauer and Yamey *op. cit.*, pp. 29-31.
[7] Federation of Malaya, *Constitutional Proposals for the Federation of Malaya* (Kuala Lumpur: Government Printer, 1957), pp. 28, 71-72.

Land Development Authority and the provision that areas of land can be scheduled for development by the Federation all help to insure that if there is vigor at the center there will be a reasonable chance of achieving development in spite of constitutional difficulties.

One special problem may, however, be foreseen. It seems clear that although technical research will be necessary, one of the great needs in agricultural development is adequate research into the motivation and social structure of the rural people. Frequent complaints about the character of Malay peasants suggest that insight into the necessary motives is still inadequate. It seems doubtful, however, whether under the Constitution Federal powers would be adequate for this work, unless it could be introduced through the Education Department.

One of the most profitable forms of development in Malaya at present would be an extension of new planting of smallholdings with modern high-yielding rubber.[8] The reasons for the emphasis on replanting have already been discussed in a previous chapter, but now that the replanting scheme is well under way new planting is likely to be expanded. Some of the great difficulties are the acute shortage of staff for agricultural work and the concentration on the opening up of rice lands. Neglect in the rural areas is closely related to the constitutional and educational pattern of Malaya, which drains away a very high proportion of the educated Malays into

[8] P. T. Bauer "Malayan Rubber Policies," *Political Science Quarterly*, LXXII (March, 1957), pp. 83-99.

administrative tasks, leaving too few for vigorous rural work. At the same time the orientation of the educational system toward English means that only people of Malay race would be likely to be of much use in development work among the smallest smallholders, who are nearly all Malay and could be instructed only by those with a really good command of the language, such as few non-Malays possess. The emphasis on Malay as a national language mainly for political reasons is likely to have some adverse effects on productivity, but in the rural areas it may help by reducing the scarcity of potential instructors.

The development of agriculture (particularly stock rearing) and of fishcries in the entrepôt ports can easily be overlooked in considering agricultural development. Production of pigs, poultry, and vegetables, as well as a marked improvement in fishing technique and equipment, appear from recent surveys to have made a substantial contribution to the prosperity of Singapore,[9] which actually exports both pig and poultry products from the island in spite of its local population of nearly a million and a half. The explanation for this is probably partly the stimulus of a rapidly expanding market with good transport and partly good veterinary work in the control of epizootics. The rate of growth of population in Singapore, however, seems likely to absorb much of the land now used for livestock in the three satellite towns which are to be built under the master plan

[9] F. C. C. Benham, *Economic Survey of Singapore* (Singapore: Government Printer, 1957).

for the island. This will certainly tend to stimulate the growth of agriculture in South Johore if conditions are allowed to develop in which the Chinese farmers from Singapore can acquire suitable land for this purpose. It is by no means certain that political conditions will allow this to happen.

Prospects for agriculture in the three Borneo territories would appear to depend to an exceptional extent on research and extension work. Soil surveys are at present being made in an effort to discover what crops would be most suitable for settled cultivation, as the tribes at present practicing shifting cultivation are induced to settle and practice a slightly less extensive form of agriculture. There can be little doubt that higher standards of living than at present could be achieved even with their existing crops by suitable agricultural extension work. Most of the land is relatively infertile, but its infertility is not so great that there can be genuine land hunger with less than one person per square mile. The need for new crops arises partly because only a comparatively dramatic increase in productivity could persuade the people to change rapidly from their present system of cultivation without a much more thorough educational effort. Some valuable social research has been done, but the educational level of the native population is hardly yet sufficiently high to make extensive use in community development work of the information derived. Rapid and considerable expansion of education is to take place in the near future in all these territories on the basis of preparatory work done since the war, but it is difficult to envisage rapid progress in agriculture until this has been carried much further.

It will be seen that development in agriculture is impeded in the Federation partly by constitutional difficulties and partly by shortage of staff, which will remedy itself in time but may take longer than Malaya can stand. In the Borneo territories the staff problems are different from those in Malaya, but the shortage of staff will also take a good deal of time to remedy.

When we turn to industrialization, we find that the scope in these areas is rather limited, but the prospects within those limits are reasonably satisfactory. Hong Kong, with its abundant enterprise and cheap skilled labor, has shown the way to quite advanced industrialization without the advantage of even as large a home market as Malaya possesses.[10] Both Hong Kong and Singapore may be adversely affected in their industrial prospects by the formation of a Common Market in Europe and its possible extension in a free-trade area. On the whole, small industrial communities of this kind can find markets more easily where tariff policies are varied and individual items may escape duty free, while a general agreement tends to introduce uniform protection at a sufficient level for industries within the area. The attitude of the Common Market to its own underdeveloped areas is liberal, and the best hope for industrialization in these small colonies, without special

[10] F. C. C. Benham, "The Growth of Manufacturing in Hong Kong," *International Affairs*, XXXII (1956), 456-463.

markets of their own, is that the free-trade area should not simply lead to a slight widening of an exclusive club, but to a generalization of the unilateral generosity of the Common Market to the manufactures of underdeveloped areas in general.

While the entrepôt ports can find small items for export to a number of small markets all over the world, based on their existing entrepôt trade, both they and the Federation will in the main have to depend on processing and finishing industries, in which they enjoy special advantages from proximity to a weight-losing material or to a market for goods which are expensive to transport in a finished condition. It seems probable that some further processing of rubber could be attempted, and certainly vegetable oils could be processed on a larger scale. It seems probable also that the fruits and spices of Malaya and the culinary skills of the local population could be used to expand the existing canning industries. Moreover, given suitable transport and institutional arrangements, the final stages of manufacture and the servicing of mechanical equipment for Asian markets could very well develop on the basis of the considerable number of small-scale engineering works now found, particularly in Singapore.

The European agency houses have in the past initiated several industrial developments, some of which have since passed into Asian hands.[11] If their efforts could be devoted increasingly to making a

[11] See G. C. Allen and Audrey G. Donnithorne, *Western Enterprise in Indonesia and Malaya* (New York: Macmillan, 1957), for examples, especially pp. 49-66.

capital profit out of pioneering such industries and selling them off to local companies, this might well provide an important continuing function for several decades for these establishments.

One difficulty which small industrial areas in underdeveloped countries tend to encounter is that because their basic products fluctuate in price and their market conditions involve great uncertainty, entrepreneurs tend to take very short views, and at the same time the periods when local development of industry seems most profitable are periods when labor is being absorbed in the agricultural and mining industries. Substantial overseas assets need to be accumulated abroad in boom times and used for development in depressions when labor is released by a low price of the export products. This is a task which the agency houses have fulfilled to some extent, except that they do not in the main try to take capital profits in boom years by selling off their undertakings to local syndicates and making plans for fresh development when labor is again available. Indeed, to some extent the European agency houses have acquired existing properties in times of low prices, so supporting a higher standard of consumption than could otherwise have been afforded at such times and rendering the economy even more dependent on overseas shareholders.

It is a difficult task to create the conditions in which new enterprises can be established when labor is available and the level of prosperity low. Where the market is as large as that of Indonesia the government can do something by tariff protection and similar measures, as was shown by the Dutch in the 1930's.[12] Economies depending on foreign markets might be able to use export subsidies financed from taxation in years of high prices, but this could be done only if the climate of international opinion was favorable, so that special exemptions were given and retaliation was not encountered.

The International Bank Mission recommended special assistance to encourage the growth of locally owned medium-scale industries based on the existing small enterprises.[13] Provision has been made for industrial research, and an institution has been established to grant small development loans. There has, however, been little organized research into the methods of growth of local business, such as might form a basis for appropriate business training. This is a task which we would like to undertake in our own university in Singapore.

One of the key factors in the growth of local businesses is the credit structure, by which I mean to cover the whole range from the supply of currency to the local capital market. In the nineteenth century the Straits Settlements experienced considerable difficulties in the establishment of a satisfactory currency,[14] but for over fifty years these difficulties have been forgotten, and the local dollar, linked first to gold and then to sterling, has been a strong currency.

[12] *Ibid.*, pp. 35-37, 257-260.

[13] International Bank for Reconstruction and Development, *op. cit.*, pp. 85-90, 305-314.

[14] J. O. Anthonisz, *Currency Reform in the Straits Settlements* (London: R. W. Simpson, n. d.).

The banking habit is also well developed in Malaya.[15] More than half the money circulating is bank money, and this probably greatly underestimates the importance of the banks in actual transactions. We can estimate fairly accurately the cash in the hands of the public in Malaya and the demand deposits in the banks, but we know virtually nothing about the rate of circulation of the currency. The rate of turnover of bank deposits is phenomenally high, even by the standards of Western countries, and approaches the rate of turnover of once a week. Wages, however, are commonly paid monthly and never more often than fortnightly, and a fairly high proportion of foodstuffs is paid for only once a month. Thus, the proportion of transactions paid for by bank money is likely to be very much higher than the proportion of bank money to the currency in circulation.

This means that the control of credit is exceptionally important, and until very recently very little official control was exercised. I have explained in an earlier chapter how the economic system stabilized itself by methods which were not dependent on official government control. In the context of currency it may be worth commenting that government budget surpluses did not merely operate directly on incomes in times of high prices, but that insofar as they were held in reserve funds in London they diminished the liquidity of the banks and so probably helped to squeeze credit also. Nevertheless, this was a largely accidental process, and the banks did not

[15] P. A. Wilson, "Money in Malaya," *Malayan Economic Review*, II (1957), pp. 53-66.

even operate on any fixed liquidity ratio and were not required to publish local returns.

The credit system does not, however, fulfil only the function of macro-economic control of the country's economy. A good credit system can also help materially in the process of concentrating resources in the hands of those most capable of using them profitably. A good credit system enables a successful businessman to make capital gains by raising the value of assets constructed with borrowed money. Without a good credit system the saving of the necessary capital may take decades, and those who achieve success will have to combine ability with a high degree of thrift. The availability of enterprise in some cultures and its lack in others is often regarded as rather mysterious, but in relation to underdeveloped countries it is worth emphasizing that enterprise is learned by experience and is stimulated by conditions in which rapid growth is possible. One of the most important conditions of rapid growth is a flexible credit system, which gives the successful businessman access to increased funds. In addition, it must be stressed that the credit system can be a fruitful source of contact with foreign countries, though it may also carry great dangers of economic dependence.

It is to be hoped that Malaya will solve the problem of the currency that is to circulate throughout the territory and will succeed in achieving coordinated central bank policy. The link with sterling will probably be a protection to Malaya, at least during the first few years of independence, in spite of the fact that Malaya has a markedly favorable balance of payments with the dollar area and helps to feed the sterling area's dollar pool. The reason for this is that the economy is strongly oriented toward international trade, and a large part of the economy is under the control of people either with no Malayan domicile or at least with no certainty of retaining it. Any doubts that assets would cease to be transferable would lead to considerable capital flight, and the effort to control short-term capital movements would do disproportionate damage to the trade of Malaya and use up an excessive proportion of its limited resources of administrative skill.

It does not follow, however, that the link with sterling implies a complete absence of control over the exchange banks. It is a matter of considerable importance that a local money market should develop, and the creation of such a market in Malaya will depend on diverting an increasing proportion of the short-term funds of the Malayan banking system to short-term investments in Malaya itself. It is to be hoped that the Central Bank will have the constitutional powers and also a sufficient staff trained to use these powers, so as to force the pace of development of a local money market.[16]

In addition to its direct advantages a local money market would help indirectly in the expansion of the local market for long-term capital. The develop-

[16] P. W. Sherwood, "The Watson-Caine Report on the Establishment of a Central Bank in Malaya," *Malayan Economic Review*, II (April, 1957), 23-34.

ment of such a capital market can be influenced by the government both through administrative action, such as the establishment of institutions for lending to industry and agriculture, and sustained efforts to float local loans in a form that will attract the savings of the public. The government can also use legislation in consultation with local business houses, insurance companies, etc., which could generate greater confidence in local dealings in shares, and it could perhaps establish a formal stock exchange. This development could, however, be materially assisted also by the agency houses themselves through systematic attempts to establish subsidiaries which could be held by local shareholders, and by diverting some of their effort and local training into the quest for capital gains along these lines.

One of the chief difficulties in the establishment of a capital market may be differences of opinion between the Federation of Malaya and Singapore. Without active participation by Chinese capitalists no effective market can develop, and a capital market with formal institutions would in fact offer greater hopes of Malayan participation than the existing capital structure of the Chinese community, which is so closely linked to family and social contacts that non-Chinese are almost wholly excluded. It will be an obvious temptation, however, for a right-wing government in Malaya which is fairly sympathetic toward foreign capital to play on European fears of left-wing government in Singapore and attempt to develop a capital market in Kuala Lumpur. It is unlikely that any such attempt would succeed, but it would carry serious dangers of a split between Chinese and non-Chinese capital, which would seriously hinder development of the whole region.

This introduces the complex question of changes in social values required for economic growth. At present the desire for improved economic conditions is widespread in Malaya, and the rapid achievement of independence has led to an expectation of change in the way of life and some willingness to accept it. There is, however, no very clear recognition of the changes in values which may be necessary in order to achieve this objective. The basic Malay culture is the culture derived originally from India and from the later impact of Islam and modified by the nature of the territory into a form in which the traders and those with external contacts were the ruling group, so that the resulting structure contained a fusion of feudalism and piracy as the basis of its economy.[17] Interwoven with this Malay pattern is that of the overseas Chinese, who have covered Southeast Asia with a network of trading and social relationships based on family, clan, or common origin, and on adaptation to the environment and mutual cohesion.[18]

[17] B. M. M. Vlekke, *Nusantara: A History of the East Indian Archipelago* (Cambridge, Mass.: Harvard University Press, 1944).
[18] V. W. W. Purcell, *The Chinese in Southeast Asia* (Oxford: Oxford University Press, 1951), especially pp. 656-662; G. W. Skinner, *Report on the Chinese in Southeast Asia* (Cornell University Southeast Asia Program, Data Paper No. 1, 1950); G. W. Skinner, "Chinese Assimilation and Thai Politics," *Journal of Asian Studies*, XVI (1957), 237-250; J-K T'ien, *The Chinese of Sarawak* (New York: Humanities Press, 1957).

These basic patterns of thought have been strongly modified by Western business practice and scientific training. Economic thinking is also influenced by nationalism from India and socialism from China. There is some recognition that change is taking place and that certain changes are necessary for economic development. Perhaps the changes in other community values are those most commonly seen to be necessary—for example, Chinese recognition that Malays must become more prudent and enterprising, and Malay recognition that Chinese must be more willing to accept the priority of the national interest over family loyalties. Because of the comparatively smooth progress toward independence there has probably been even less thought than in other Asian countries about the changes in attitude and character needed for rapid economic and political development.

The contrast in the attitudes of nationalist intellectuals of the different Asian countries to Western values is a fascinating topic, but one which I cannot develop here. Generally speaking, there are traces in Malaya of the attitude that the British have kept the Malays backward by a system of indirect rule which did not allow them full access to modern Western civilization, an attitude which has something in common with that of Indonesian nationalists, but there is also some tendency to react in favor of a vaguely Asian culture against Western economic and political institutions. But it is not easy to see any evidence of positive proposals for change, still less of any recognition that such changes may be related to the possibilities of economic development.

When the subject of changes in social values is raised at all, economists usually tend to emphasize the need for encouraging enterprise and keeping out of its way. Whether this is what is needed in other underdeveloped countries I would not venture to say. It does not seem to me to be the chief need in Malaya. The Europeans may be more enterprising in this sense than the Malays, though even this cannot be taken for granted when the extraordinary change in Malay patterns of life within seventy-five years is taken into account. But Europeans are certainly not more enterprising than Chinese. European business institutions have been able to survive and grow in spite of higher costs because of a flexible formal structure within which individuals are content to seek advantage by playing assigned roles. The formal structure with its instruments for finance, investigation, risk bearing, and other objects has been better able to acquire and use new knowledge than the equally enterprising but more personal and informal Chinese structure.

This tendency to play assigned roles within institutions is something akin to professionalism, though its range is rather wider. Not all the posts in European firms involve technical professional training, but most of them involve something more than specialization. The relationship to the whole institution is something that is usually not entirely rigid: in a sense the individual makes his own position, but this is normally merely a flexibility within a fairly definite formal structure. It is the comparative absence of this formal structure within the traditional forms of business in Malaya which prevents most of the Chinese businesses from expanding to any considerable size. This is often expressed crudely in such statements as that the Chinese cannot trust one another with responsibility, but it would probably be true to say that Chinese business is characterized by at least as much mutual trust based on social relations as European business. The essential difference is more nearly that the different individuals are to a greater extent trying to do the same thing, each in business for an individual profit within a given social framework, rather than each playing an assigned role within an organization, the growth of which will benefit all. I have expressed this elsewhere[19] by suggesting that Malaya suffers from an excess rather than a deficiency of enterprise. Private enterprise indeed seems to work best when the entrepreneurial function itself is specialized, and not too widely diffused.

In this respect the role of trade associations might well be more important than it actually is. Several of the associations have run into racial difficulties, either open or concealed, and in one or two instances associations which were primarily technical and professional before the war were converted by the postwar inflation and the growth of trade unionism into little more than trade unions with quite rudimentary professional functions. Both the gov-

[19] T. H. Silcock, *The Economy of Malaya* (Singapore: Donald Moore, 1954), p. 44.

ernment and the university have attempted to encourage and assist the growth of professional organizations, and much valuable work has been done in the last few years in the commercial firms in stimulating junior professional organizations. A few craft unions also exist, based on traditional Chinese guilds, but much more has been done to encourage their negotiating and organizing activities than to give them responsibility for standards and techniques.

I should not wish it to be understood from this that I regard Malaya as backward in promoting activity of this kind, in comparison with other underdeveloped countries. The opportunities in Malaya, however, seem to be unusually good because there is a strong guild tradition among the Chinese who form the majority in most skilled trades, and because there is already a fairly strong basis of trade unionism. The subject is one on which useful sociological research might be done in other underdeveloped countries, and in which economists should certainly take an interest.

Professional associations are probably one of the principal channels by which standards and a professional spirit are cultivated. It is not, however, sufficiently realized that a relation exists between economic development and the virtues and vices which an educational system develops. A certain minimum of public spirit and reliability in fulfilling obligations which have no moral sanction beyond being obligations would appear to be requisites, and we might regard these as virtues that should be stimulated.

On the other hand, preoccupation with time and measurement and a competitive spirit are also valuable in economic development, but many would regard these not as virtues to be inculcated but as vices attendant on our Western social structure. In most underdeveloped countries there is much discussion both of economic development and of education, but outside Communist countries little attention is paid to the relation between the attitudes fostered by education and the attitudes needed for rapid economic growth.

In Malaya the discussion of education is primarily concerned with nation building, and the chief point at issue is language and a common Malayan outlook. A subsidiary point is the development of technology, and there is also discussion of civic and religious education, yet economic progress is certainly desired, and the International Bank Mission report emphasizes the need for creating conditions in which Malaya's many small businesses can grow to intermediate size. Some of the necessary qualities may be incidental results of civic or religious education, but the matter is at least worthy of attention.

This is not a suitable occasion for discussing Malaya's language problems, but some of them have important implications both for attitudes and for technology. Broadly speaking, the majority of the electorate, including many of the politically conscious non-Malays, desire to emphasize Malay as a medium of instruction for the sake of nation-building. English, on the other hand, is still mainly desired by individual parents for their children on economic grounds. Insofar as Malay is not accepted by individuals in their non-political capacity, the use of Malay would tend to hamper development simply by holding back education, but the problem of the use of English or of the vernacular is one which is relevant in all underdeveloped countries and in which the size of the country and its existing language pattern may create relevant differences between different countries.

Up to a certain level of skill it is extremely wasteful and costly to use as a medium of instruction any language other than a vernacular. It is clearly much cheaper to translate the necessary texts and teaching methods into terms acceptable to the local culture than to train large numbers of not very able pupils in foreign-language skills. As economists, however, we should draw attention to the fact that there are economies of scale in the production of textbooks and manuals and that, therefore, the appropriate level of skill to be inculcated through any given vernacular depends in part on its size. Insofar as Malay is assimilated to Bahasa Indonesia it ranks as a comparatively widely spoken language, though, of course, both the Chinese National Language and Tamil have similar claims, and the national arguments against them apply also against making Malay more like the language of its neighbor to the south. Probably all of the existing underdeveloped countries, with the possible exception of China, will need to have a substantial part of their postsecondary education in a foreign language for several decades to come. The relations between such education and the stimulation of research and technical training have important economic implications which economists should keep in view. In Malaya, as in other underdeveloped countries, they are likely to occupy a subsidiary place in public attention.

The last of the development needs which we promised to consider was that for research and technical assistance. These are not synonymous, but it is useful to consider them together. Few underdeveloped countries can achieve very much research without outside assistance, and outside assistance without research is likely to lead to wasteful copying of irrelevant foreign techniques. The reason why underdeveloped countries will be unlikely to produce much research without outside assistance is that research as a specialist activity is very costly and as an auxiliary activity in universities it is likely to suffer both from the very rapid expansion of student numbers that is necessary and from the increasing use of academic consultants from the universities by many governments of underdeveloped countries. In my work on behalf of the Research Liaison Centre for Economics Departments in Southeast Asia I have encountered this pressure on the time of senior academic staff in nearly all the universities.

It should not be necessary to emphasize that technical assistance without research will lead to wasteful copying. Economists are familiar with the fact that labor, capital, and different skills are not uniformly scarce in all countries and that appropriate techniques should allow for this. Yet the individuals who are required to make these allowances are usually either young men who have specialized wholly on foreign technique or visiting experts with an assignment of one or two years. Colonial officials are often amateurs in the techniques that they introduce, but the mere fact that their length of tenure obliges them to be familiar with two systems of thought probably makes them rather less wasteful than either of the two classes I have mentioned. But colonial officials are a dying race, and in the preceding chapter I have already drawn attention to the tendency to improvise for the colonial system itself rather than for development.

We therefore have a situation in which research is likely to be neglected and is also exceptionally important. A few of the important economic fields in which research would certainly help are economic research into trade policy (particularly regional relations among underdeveloped countries), economic research into currency problems, research into the adaptation of business techniques, social as well as technical research as the basis for agricultural extension work and community development, and, perhaps most important of all, social research on acceptance of birth-control techniques as a basis for population policy. I have mentioned, of course, only the research in economic or allied fields, but a very great extension in almost every field would prevent the waste of funds being used for technical assistance.

Probably much more could be done to promote research contacts between universities in developed and underdeveloped countries. The great American area-studies programs and some of the contracts given to universities under your government's foreign aid program have given a lead in this respect; in the United Kingdom we have the Inter-University Council for Higher Education Overseas, and in our Singapore Liaison Centre we are trying to arrange for research contact in our own field between the universities of Southeast Asia and the economic research institutes of Europe.

One of the chief arguments in favor of organizing a development fund through the United Nations is that it would enable research to be financed by the wealthiest countries, while the specialist talents needed could be drawn from any country in which they were found.

In Malaya we are very conscious that our research still falls far short of what is needed. The governments on the whole are generous with funds, but there is such a shortage of really able trained men for the government services that it is extremely difficult to get the necessary personnel. The feeling that foreign techniques are imported by colonial regimes without sufficient adaptation to the local environment is very strong among the intellectuals of most of the countries which have recently emerged from colonialism. This greatly underestimates the inventiveness of many colonial systems, but it provides a favorable climate for research, and a great deal more could certainly be done.

The Commonwealth provides one of the links by which research can be maintained and encouraged, but there are many other roles which it can play in encouraging Malaya's economic development. I shall discuss here the help which Malaya can derive from its membership in the Commonwealth in its political, financial, and commercial relations and also the Commonwealth's role as a challenge and as a possible medium for development activities.

Politically, the principal help that Malaya's economy derives from its membership in the Commonwealth is the possibility of building up diplomatic relations gradually. The transition from dependence to independence must inevitably at some point be sudden. Sovereignty must at some stage be acquired, but with membership of the Commonwealth it is possible to maintain continuity to a much greater extent than would be possible without it. Malaya can concentrate its limited corps of trained diplomats in the few places where special policy problems are involved and continue to make use of many of the services of the United Kingdom where policy issues do not arise. Other newly independent countries, even larger than Malaya, are severely handicapped in ordinary relations with foreign countries by under-staffing, either in quality or in quantity or both, of their overseas service. There is no reason to suppose that Malaya will lose any independence of action by making use of these contacts, since independent representatives can be appointed wherever any purpose is served by doing so. Yet, if it enables Malaya to maintain a first-class service overseas without undue strain on its economy, this should give it access to a great deal of foreign assistance and enable it to use to the full whatever influence and bargaining power a small country is in a position to wield.

Participation in the Commonwealth Prime Ministers' Conference and in the Commonwealth joint activities will be valued by Malaya, chiefly because the Commonwealth makes possible mutual interpretation of developed and underdeveloped countries. Just as India has a role in the Commonwealth as an interpreter of Afro-Asian views on a large number of issues, Malaya will be able to express the view of the smaller underdeveloped countries within the Commonwealth gatherings; for Malaya is one of a group of Southeast Asian countries which are all fairly small and which differ sharply in their political contacts but are increasingly conscious of common interests based on their geographical position, their economic characteristics, and their size. In a sense the Commonwealth is more than a meeting place of the countries involved and plays the role of an institution in which foreign policy problems involving a number of different interests can be worked out with mutual confidence.

The most important financial feature of Malaya's membership in the Commonwealth will be its continuing membership in the sterling area system. The two are not, of course, entirely synonymous since we have seen that Burma retains important links with sterling but not with the Commonwealth, while Canada is in the converse position.

It is worthy of emphasis that during 1958 we have seen a significant change in the position of the sterling area, by virtue of the independence of Ghana and Malaya. It has been argued in the past[20] that the sterling area was held together by the fact that Britain exercised political control over the colonial territories, which on balance enjoyed a substantially favorable balance of payments with the dollar area, and that this made it possible for a number of independent currencies of varying degrees of hardness all to have an interest in belonging to a single currency area. In Europe, the United States had to provide the necessary dollar credits to set in motion the liberalizing movement which has now led to the Common Market. Weaker countries within the sterling area, while theoretically seeing the advantage of a single currency area, might feel that they had to protect themselves against stronger currencies by devices which would ultimately break up the system. The thing that was believed to prevent this was the favorable balances of the colonies.

The problem will now arise whether with Ghana and Malaya independent the sterling area can still hold together, for without these two countries the colonies will offer a negligible bait to the independent Commonwealth countries. Will Ghana and Ma-

[20] Judd Polk, *Sterling, Its Meaning in World Finance* (New York: Harper Bros., 1956), pp. 175-207, 227-232.

laya feel that their own best interest will be served
by allowing the strength of their own currencies to
secure them imports on favorable terms from all
countries? And will this lead to an unwillingness of
other Commonwealth countries to surrender their
dollar earnings and their freedom of action in foreign
exchange matters with no other advantage than the
international contacts of the sterling area?

I am in no position to prophesy what will happen
in Ghana, and even in Malaya it is never possible
to be certain. It seems likely, however, that Malaya
will wish to remain a sterling country and accept
the obligation to contribute its dollar earnings to the
pool and to co-ordinate in some degree its exchange-
control policy. In part, advantages that Malaya will
derive from this lie in the greater sense of security of the capitalists who own a large share of
Malaya's trading assets and could not be prevented
from transferring them elsewhere without serious
damage to the economy. There is also the advantage
that membership in the sterling area system may give
access to both short-term and long-term capital. The
former is likely to be more important to the Federation, the latter to Singapore, though the amount of
capital which could be made available from Malayan
sources by suitable financial institutions ought not to
be underestimated. One further advantage is that
the very large variations in foreign balances that Malaya will need as a result of the great fluctuations in
tin and rubber prices will be easier as part of an automatic system than they would be at present for an

independent Central Bank. In principle, of course, the government could build up substantial foreign reserves at certain times and run them down at others without belonging to the sterling area system, but politicians may well feel that the sterling area is some protection to them in dealing with the fluctuations of Malaya's national income.

Malaya probably contributes much more to the sterling area system than it gains from it, and this should be a source of bargaining power in the future, but it is not easy to see how Malaya could in fact do better on an independent currency system.

In commercial policy the Commonwealth can remain an instrument for fostering trade between developed and underdeveloped countries. It has recently been pointed out[21] that this trade is declining in relative importance in the world, and the increases in international trade have been among the more developed countries themselves. It is suggested that this is mainly because chemistry and new technologies have reduced the importance of exotic plants dependent on unique climates. The Commonwealth preference system does a little to promote exchanges between the developed and underdeveloped countries within the Commonwealth itself, but it should do much more than this if it is really to play an important role in commercial policy. No coordinated policy has been worked out for making the Commonwealth market an instrument of eco-

[21] R. Nurkse, "Excess Population and Capital Construction," *Malayan Economic Review*, II (1957), 10.

nomic development for the less developed sections. Indeed, competition from Commonwealth industries with low labor costs might well be resented in parts of the Commonwealth where these costs are higher. Yet, unless the Commonwealth countries with relatively low wages can develop their industries in relation to a broad market their wage conditions are unlikely to improve. Unilateral trade concessions for underdeveloped countries could be very important instruments of development and could help to discourage the tendency to think of development as a closed-economy problem. Malaya as an underdeveloped country with a relatively open economy would be likely to welcome measures designed to foster development through trade preference.

It should be emphasized that what is needed is not simply a greater freeing of trade. The real problem is that there are a large number of underdeveloped countries, each of which individually has a small home market, which need to foster trade among themselves and at the same time to protect themselves against the competition of more highly developed industrial economies. Most of these countries have too little in common to arrange large-scale customs unions, and the limited concessions which they could make to one another would normally conflict with the provisions of the General Agreement on Tariffs and Trade. This is a situation in which an enthusiastically liberal attitude towards underdeveloped countries is required. The Commonwealth has not, up to the present, given any example of such an attitude, and indeed the approach of the six countries of the European Common Market to the economies of their overseas territories is in many ways more liberal than anything which the Commonwealth has yet achieved in this sphere. The common institutions of the Commonwealth may, however, provide a framework of discussion in which the spirit of the Colombo Plan could be applied to trade policy between developed and underdeveloped countries.

The Commonwealth can also play an important role in helping the cultural changes which will be needed for economic development. Membership in the Commonwealth is unlikely to persist in any countries in which the leadership is not in some sense held by Western-educated classes which are trying to initiate cultural changes. In a sense the Commonwealth can help these groups to retain leadership in their countries, but the difficulty of the position should not be neglected. It is essential that membership in the Commonwealth should not appear to be something which supports any one group by outside power or influence. It must be a means by which these people can be assisted in carrying out objectives which their own populations desire, in a way which would not be available without it. So long as the Western-educated leaders can secure real advantages which help in development, they may be assisted in achieving their own objectives, which at present do not command widespread popular support.

On the one hand the Commonwealth can give

access to technical assistance and to professional, academic, and scientific bodies in the outside world; on the other it can stimulate the desire to achieve parity in standards which the leaders themselves may feel are important, either in themselves or for economic development, but which without membership in the Commonwealth might appear merely to be relics of colonialism. The rule of law, academic freedom, humane standards in social services, and scientific integrity are all probably valued by a substantial section of the intellectuals in underdeveloped countries, but their power to influence their electorates in favor of these things depends largely on participation in Commonwealth and other international institutions in which these things are expected, and which stand for opportunity in the minds of the public.

The leaders of countries like Malaya and Singapore are at present people with Western education, though not, of course, with a wholly Western outlook. They must work on behalf of their own peoples, but they are likely to be greatly assisted by recognition, both of their responsibility and of their difficulties, by more developed states which can nevertheless treat them as equals. It is not impossible that international agencies like the Economic Commission for Asia and the Far East and the Economic Commission for Africa (when it comes into existence) will have a similar effect, but these bodies are almost in principle opposed to recognizing as desirable any standards which are not common to all members.

Some of the important tasks which the Commonwealth could undertake in development planning are: first, the continuation of the excellent work of the Colombo Plan; next, some organization of migration wherever possibilities exist and study of some of the more difficult implications of migration; next, some further development of organs for consultation below the prime minister level on development problems which are shared among different Commonwealth countries; and, finally, perhaps a Commonwealth program in public utilities. We can discuss these points a little more fully.

The Colombo Plan is often represented as chiefly a channel for aid from the more developed to the less developed Commonwealth countries. It is, however, very much more than this, and indeed much of the international aid which is listed in Colombo Plan reports would in fact have been available if the Colombo Plan had never existed.[22] The chief importance of the Plan is that it has enabled a group of Commonwealth and other countries to coordinate their development needs and to stimulate one another to detailed analysis of what those needs are.

Common discussion of these problems among co-operative politicians and civil servants has com-

[22] The report published in Singapore, for example, lists private investments by the United Kingdom and the United States, loans by the U. S. Export-Import Bank and the International Bank for Reconstruction and Development, and even drawings by Southeast Asian countries on their sterling balances (The Colombo Plan, *Fourth Annual Report*, Singapore: Government Printer, 1955, pp. 160-169).

pletely transformed the atmosphere and fostered much greater willingness to receive, to give, and, above all, to accept and offer advice. A good deal has been done in fostering technical training, and it is noteworthy that India, which is not a wealthy country but which enjoys certain technical advantages by virtue of its size and long association with Western technology, has itself been able to offer technical assistance in certain fields to other underdeveloped countries. This process of association and regular discussion needs to be expanded, and it is to be hoped that the United States will take an increasing part in the discussions and exchanges of ideas, which are among the most important features of this Commonwealth institution.

Migration within the Commonwealth is apt to be a rather sore subject because different Commonwealth countries feel it necessary to restrict immigration from other Commonwealth countries on the ground that immigration might be economically, culturally, or politically harmful. Nevertheless, the Commonwealth is a great laboratory of immigration practices, and more pooling of ideas on the subject should be beneficial. In the nineteenth century the form of migration which received most attention was that of free migrants from developed countries for settlement in relatively empty countries such as Canada or Australia. During this period, however, there was also a great deal of migration taking place under conditions of indenture or controlled or assisted passages into Malaya and Ceylon and out of India;

there was also a great deal of migration of business and professional men, civil servants, and the like from the United Kingdom to dependent countries.

This migration formed the basis of much of the population and indeed much of the economy and the culture of large parts of the Commonwealth. A great deal of advantage could accrue from investigations of the economic and social implications of these migrations and the way in which they are related to training. The complex relations between economic and political status; the influences of migration on the technique of training and the attitude to it; and questions of assimilation, cultural interactions, and repatriation, are all matters which could well be studied on a Commonwealth basis with profit to different Commonwealth countries and probable removal of avoidable misunderstandings. Malaya has many migration problems, including techniques of assimilation, relations with the country of origin, and the role of such specialist migrants as Europeans and Japanese. It is to be hoped that the development of Commonwealth studies will include studies of migration by economic and sociological techniques.

The Commonwealth has always carefully avoided institutions on a supernational level, but in the sphere of economic development it may be worth considering more systematic consultation among other specialist ministers below the level of the Prime Ministers' Conference. The forthcoming economic conference may perhaps recommend regular technical

consultations on economic matters where policy differences are unlikely to be important, and it would
certainly seem advantageous to have some exchange
among junior ministers or civil servants with similar
interests. These conferences would be advantageous
wherever policy agreement had been achieved and
the development of regulations or administrative
action required co-ordination among more than two
different governments.

The final role that the Commonwealth might
well attempt to play in development is the working
out of more thorough-going transport plans on a
Commonwealth basis. In the nineteenth century
the chief forms of transport development were railway building and the construction of ports. The
former could be organized largely on a private
basis through the City of London, though the latter
was commonly in part a public undertaking. At the
present time road development is one of the most
important sources of economic growth and is something which for technical reasons has to be almost
wholly undertaken by governments. In some cases
co-operation in research on both the technique and
the social and economic implications of road building
could be helpful to the poorer Commonwealth territories, but the help of Commonwealth countries in
the general planning and financing of transport
would almost certainly be a useful stimulus to development. In the Southeast Asia area the chief need
is for more co-operation between the three Borneo
territories and Malaya, but it seems unlikely that this

would come about except as part of a wider Commonwealth transport development plan.

Some of these comments on possible Commonwealth developments may seem rather vague wishful thinking. It is time to turn to possible influences of American scholars and the American public on Commonwealth development, as seen from the point of view of Southeast Asia.

In the first volume in this series Professor Underhill[23] drew attention to an American contribution which was increasingly being made to the Commonwealth. Since he is a Canadian, Professor Underhill's emphasis was primarily on the contribution to the part of the Commonwealth which consists of people of European stock. Looking at it from Malaya, I feel that there is a contribution which is being made and can be made on a much larger scale to the Commonwealth as a bridge between countries of European stock and underdeveloped countries which were previously colonies. The liquidation of colonialism leaves more difficult problems in these countries, and the contribution which the United States can make is not one of showing the way in terms of its own experience. I should say rather that American presuppositions (or should we call them prejudices?) are complementary to British ones, and that, therefore, we can learn something from one another in tackling our modern problems.

We can draw attention to these different presup-

[23] F. H. Underhill, *The British Commonwealth* (Durham, N. C.: Duke University Press, 1956), pp. 99-101.

positions by considering the attitudes of the two countries to the relation of America to the Commonwealth itself. Broadly, the average Englishman would probably feel that the separation of the United States from the Commonwealth was in a sense a regrettable accident due to bungling by George III and his Cabinet and hasty tempers across the Atlantic. Subsequent developments in Canada and Australia have indicated that the break was quite unnecessary, and the Commonwealth would be much more of a reality if it had remained united and the overseas territories had by now become much the most important part of the whole institution.

I believe there would be very few Americans who could subscribe to such an attitude. It might be fair to suggest that they feel that the British mended their ways to some extent in the nineteenth century in dealing with people of their own race as a result of sharp lessons administered by the United States; and that successful pressure by India, with a good deal of American aid, helped to induce a similar reform toward the more developed non-European areas after the Second World War. Even so, Britain still remains a colonial power and on that account is mistrusted in its dealings, particularly with underdeveloped countries.

It is not helpful to deal with myths of this kind merely by asking how far they are true. Clearly they are both oversimplifications of situations that inevitably arise when a country with superior political and economic power comes into close trading or cultural contact with other countries. British people have been emigrants for many reasons for rather more than three hundred years, and they have migrated both to countries where the local population was negligible and to countries in which Europeans could never hope to be more than a small minority. The United States arose as a result of a revolt of one of these groups of migrants, and it is predominantly an immigrant country whose people are normally averse to staying abroad for long periods. Both countries have had trading and political relations all over the world, and both have found the superior political and economic power of their government involved rather against their will in political situations in other parts of the world. The preconceptions of the two countries result in their handling these situations differently; in particular there is rarely a permanent or semipermanent group of Americans on the spot in any overseas territory where United States interests are involved.

The United States believes strongly in not interfering. We all know that it is impossible to give money or material goods as charity without influencing the behavior of the recipients, but it is possible, given good will and intelligence, to make such interference constructive and to prevent its being resented. I believe that British people tend to feel that it is refusing to face the facts if one aims at keeping one's impacts to a minimum and that the aim should be to use power constructively.

Because British people have been emigrants and

have had long experience in dealing with distant countries during a time when communications were poor, we have had a much stronger tendency to trust the man on the spot and also to emphasize cultural differences between ourselves and other peoples. Americans, who have been outstandingly successful in assimilating immigrants from so many countries, are more apt to treat the local populations as similar to themselves and likely to behave correctly if given similar institutions.

Perhaps this is caricaturing the situation slightly, but in drawing attention to these differences of attitude I want to make the point that the colonial influences to which Americans object in British relations with territories inhabited by non-British people are quite genuine things which need to be resisted; but that they are not a result of British hypocrisy but of the role played by the man on the spot in a situation where migrants are few and powerful and can often involve their home government in protecting their interests.

Some years ago an American scholar visiting Southeast Asia, in the days when it was still fashionable to make such study tours occasions for pin-pointing some of the detailed evils of colonialism, explained to me that it was unfair to judge the attitude of the American people to Japan in terms of the policies planned by officials on the spot, still less the policies carried out by their subordinates, because these people had special interests of their own in Japan. I remember thinking that foreign travel was an educative experience and that in time the moral of the story would be learned. I should like to be able to say that I refrained from pointing the moral, but honesty compels me to admit that I started talking as a representative of one colonial power to the representative of another.

As I have indicated, we are both inevitably involved in power situations overseas, and a little fun can be derived from drawing these parallels. The differences, however, are very much more important than the similarities. It is this that makes American relations with the Commonwealth important, partly because basic American attitudes can be a useful stimulus, both to us in our dealings with areas that are still colonies, and to the leaders of the ex-colonies which are now the non-European members of the Commonwealth. I should like to conclude by mentioning four respects in which the differences in attitude can be specially helpful.

First of all, because Americans do not live overseas for long periods, they have found it necessary increasingly to rely on research for basic information about the different countries with which they have relations. It can be argued that it is as unhealthy to trust the judgment of a specialist research worker who has studied one problem for two or three years as to trust that of a colonial administrator who is something of an amateur in every aspect of the country and has had time to acquire many vested interests. I should not like to argue this point at length but would emphasize that at the very least the presence of large numbers of research workers helps enormously, both to keep the administrator objective and to weaken any tendency to protect vested interests by arguing that those who do not share them do not know the country.

I have already indicated that there is scope for a great deal of research in stimulating economic development and would urge that the number of American research workers in the field should be greatly expanded. It would be surprising if American funds were not now being wasted for lack of information. A large overseas civil service is costly, but to get the same amount of necessary information from research workers must necessarily be much more costly. Possibly the information derived is better, but no one can pretend that it should be cheap. I would make a special plea for research in the colonial or newly independent countries of the Commonwealth, where there is likely to be a great dearth of local knowledge partly because of distrust of colonial officials, partly because of their departure, and partly because of the various factors I have already mentioned which limit the amount of research which is likely to be done in these areas without aid.

I have mentioned the possibility of expanded studies of migration. Studies either historical or sociological of the European communities in the various predominantly non-European areas on a comparative basis might yield much useful information, and I feel that if it were done by American scholars of the present vintage—as distinct from those of the late prewar and early postwar periods—it could promote Anglo-American understanding in a field where differences of opinion are only too probable.

A second point in which American public opinion might assist the Commonwealth, and perhaps also be assisted by it, is the provision of unconditional aid to independent countries. Both British and European opinion appears to be moving in the direction of accepting responsibility for some such aid. It would be possible for Americans to check this tendency by taking the view that defense or other help from the United States ought not to be given to any countries which could afford to give foreign aid themselves. This might be particularly likely if there were differences of opinion concerning the channels through which aid should be given.

It would probably be helpful if the United States could emphasize the possibility of giving aid without political conditions since the British attitude seems rather excessively preoccupied with the view that any direct aid from one country to another necessarily interferes with the latter's independence.

A third respect in which the United States could assist the Commonwealth is in not pressing too hard the argument in favor of non-discrimination in trade. It is very much to be hoped that the generous attitude of the countries of the European Common Market to their overseas territories will generate a similar attitude by the United Kingdom towards underdeveloped countries in general in the free-trade area negotiations. American opinion might easily object to waiving the rules of G.A.T.T. in favor of countries with low wages on the ground that it would help their development. It may be impossible for the United States with its own protective policy to make similar concessions—which would, of course, be one of the most striking ways in which the United States could help underdeveloped countries—but there is a danger that it would use its influence against any such one-sided liberalization merely on principle.

Finally, I believe there is considerable scope for an increase in mutual understanding between the United States and the Commonwealth in the appropriate design of education for political and economic development. Broadly speaking, the attitude of the United Kingdom towards education in underdeveloped countries has been influenced by its own educational system, which strongly emphasizes the creation of an elite. This has necessarily led to education on a rather limited scale, particularly because, as I have indicated earlier, the local British population has seen the expansion of education as rather opposed to its own interest. On the other hand, the United States has strongly emphasized education of the whole population and has also stressed technology.

In Malaya some controversy has arisen over the recognition of American degrees, which is largely based on the fact that universities in the Commonwealth are chartered institutions recognized by the local government and subjected to various tests before recognition is given. The approach in the United States is different, and there can be little doubt that in Malaya and some other places in the Commonwealth from which students can go to the United States for higher studies this system can lead to some anomalies. On the other hand too much emphasis on universal education may lead, if the population is increasing rapidly and the country is poor, to excessively low standards and a general sense of frustration. The contrast in attitudes between the Commonwealth and the United States is one which merits very full discussion, preferably in a conference or working party in which members of some of the Commonwealth underdeveloped countries and perhaps other underdeveloped countries could participate. Both the Commonwealth system and the aid programs of the United States are designed to aid development, political as well as economic, and both appear to be largely based on the systems that have grown up in very different conditions in the home countries. The design of appropriate techniques certainly needs further study.

I hope that in indicating some of the advantages that may accrue from the differences between the presuppositions of America and of the United Kingdom I shall not be taken as implying that these differences do no harm. They can, of course, be a source of misunderstanding. In particular, I fear that they will lead you to believe that I am speaking as a typical colonial exploiter trying to make colonialism sound rather respectable and not too different from what you do yourselves. And, perhaps, as an Englishman I should be led by the same differences to regret that Americans were not participating with us in this Commonwealth undertaking of development.

4

Malaya and the European Free Trade Area[1]

For the purpose of this chapter we shall mean by Malaya the Federation of Malaya and Singapore. This should not be taken as implying that the attitudes of the two territories are necessarily the same, or even that they share a common economy. The relations between the Federation of Malaya, which has just become an independent member of the Commonwealth, and Singapore, which has just secured control over its own domestic and trade policy, are undergoing marked changes, and these cannot be neglected in a study of this kind. The economy of Malaya is still, however, largely a single economy, experiencing some division as a result of political changes. Hence it is not possible to consider the impact of the European Economic Community and the Free Trade Area on the Federation of Malaya

[1] This chapter is due to appear in substantially the same form, though without notes or references, in *The Commonwealth and the European Free Trade Area* (to be published in London by the United Kingdom Council of the European Movement). My thanks are due to the United Kingdom Council of the European Movement for permission to publish it here.

alone. Even separate statistics for the Federation of Malaya are not always available.

The Federation of Malaya is a producer of primary products, chiefly rubber and tin. Its economy, during the period of colonial rule, was largely organized through distributing centers in Singapore and Penang, which were and still remain free ports doing an extensive entrepôt trade that reaches far beyond Malaya. Government opinion in Kuala Lumpur is influenced by the view that independence means an opportunity to be free of what it regards as economic control from Singapore, and this may lead to some changes in the structure of the economy. It is impossible to foretell the future relations between Singapore merchants and the Federation economy; but it would be very naïve to assume either that the existing largely Pan-Malayan structure of the economy will remain unchanged or that Singapore's trade will prove any more amenable to political intervention from Kuala Lumpur than it has to any of the numerous attempts of governments in Southeast Asia to control it, ever since the city's foundation. Thus, business is still largely Pan-Malayan, government is divided, and the situation is fluid; and Malaya's interest must be considered in this context.

The Malayan economy is a reasonably prosperous one. Income per head (gross national product) has not been calculated separately for the two territories. A recent economic survey of Singapore[2] esti-

[2] F. C. C. Benham, *Economic Survey 1957* (Singapore: Government Printer, 1957), Section 8. The definition of national income is not given for this approximate estimate.

mates about £12 per month per head for the island in 1956. The most recent figure for Malaya as a whole, in the International Bank Mission report, was about £7 per month in 1953;[3] but there has certainly been a rise since then, and the income per head in the Federation alone is probably now about £7 or rather more than half that of Singapore. Even this is high by Asian standards, possibly higher than Japan and much higher than India.

Much of this wealth is concentrated in a prosperous middle class. No other country in Asia has under 120 people per private car. Malaya as a whole has 70, Singapore under 30.[4] Peasant incomes in the villages are much lower than the national average, some £6 a month *for a family* being fairly typical.[5] Population is increasing rapidly everywhere, and neither new land settlement nor new building is keeping pace with it. Thus, there are bitter paradoxes of rural poverty in a wealthy country and rural overcrowding in a country where less than a quarter of the land is occupied. These set the problems which any Malayan government must

[3] International Bank for Reconstruction and Development, *Economic Development of Malaya*, p. 509. The figure taken is gross resident national income at factor cost.

[4] United Nations Economic Commission for Asia and the Far East, *Annual Economic Survey, 1956* (New York: United Nations, 1957), pp. 178, 182 (population figures corrected by figures from the preliminary count of the 1957 Census of Singapore, so far published only in the local press).

[5] Ungku A. Aziz, *Economic Survey of Five Villages in Nyalas, Malacca* (Kuala Lumpur: Rural and Industrial Development Authority, 1957; mimeographed; publication expected shortly).

face. Yet in spite of them Malaya is basically still a contented and tolerant place.

Tables I and II show the gross exports of Malaya to the Common Market and the other countries of the Free Trade Area respectively in 1955 and 1956. Only the countries considered as probably full mem-

TABLE I

Exports of Principal Products by Value from Malaya (the Federation of Malaya and Singapore) to Countries of the European Common Market (Belgium, France, Western Germany, Italy, Luxemburg, and the Netherlands), 1955-1956.

	Malayan $ millions	
	1955	1956
Total Exports*................	724	697
Crude Rubber..............	573	500
Tin......................	51	75
Vegetable Oils..............	22	32
Coffee....................	11	37
Pepper....................	11	10

Source: *Malayan Statistics: External Trade of Malaya, 1955, 1956* (Singapore, Registrar of Malayan Statistics). The Malayan dollar (M$) was worth $.327 U.S. (2/4 U.K.) in 1956.

* Excluding Ships and Aircraft Stores

TABLE II

Exports of Principal Products by Value from Malaya (the Federation of Malaya and Singapore) to Other Principal Countries of the Proposed European Free Trade Area (United Kingdom, Austria, Denmark, Norway, Sweden, and Switzerland) 1955-1956.

	Malayan $ millions	
	1955	1956
Total Exports*..............	801	707
Crude Rubber..............	649	567
Tin......................	20	15
Fruits, Preserved...........	26	27
Vegetable Oils..............	41	34
Pepper....................	11	13

Source: *Malayan Statistics: External Trade of Malaya, 1955, 1956* (Singapore, Registrar of Malayan Statistics).

* Excluding Ships and Aircraft Stores, Parcel Post, and Special Transactions

bers of the Free Trade Area[6] are included in Table II. Several of the goods exported are not products of Malayan origin, but re-exports in whole or in part. Because of the nature of the entrepôt trade of Singapore and Penang, re-exports are not shown separately, though approximate figures can be de-

[6] United Kingdom Council of the European Movement, *A Free Trade Area in Europe* (London: U. K. Council of the European Movement, 1957).

rived from the main tables and this information has been used in the text.

The chief exports are rubber and tin, which will be hardly affected directly by either the Customs Union or the Free Trade Area. This is not because Europe is an unimportant customer, but because, with no alternative source of supply within the Area, customs duties are relatively unimportant in this trade in two essential raw materials. The duty on rubber will be a mere 3 per cent, and tin will be duty free if unwrought and pay less than 10 per cent on some made-up items in the Common Market. The rubber duty is likely to be negligible in its effect, as price margins between natural and synthetic rubber go far beyond 3 per cent and there is no significant source of natural rubber within the Common Market. At the worst it would perhaps encourage some slight substitution of synthetic for natural rubber in the European market. It is unlikely that the tin duty will have any significant effect, though it might affect some exported items slightly. Malaya's trade classification makes this difficult to predict accurately.

About $M 500 million worth, or a quarter of Malaya's gross exports of rubber in 1956, went to the six countries of the Common Market. A further quarter went to the United Kingdom; but the combined exports to the other countries of the proposed Free Trade Area were less than 5 per cent of Malaya's gross exports of this product. Some two-fifths of rubber exports went to America and Canada.

The remainder was scattered among many different countries, Japan being the largest market.

For tin about 60 per cent by value of the gross exports of blocks, ingots, bars, and slabs went to the United States and Canada, 15 per cent to the Common Market Area, under 3 per cent to the United Kingdom and under 1 per cent to other countries of the Free Trade Area. Thus the European Common Market is an important consumer of Malaya's tin, but the integration of this market will have little direct effect.

Rubber and tin between them accounted for about four-fifths of Malaya's total gross exports to the Common Market area in 1956, and this year was not exceptional, though of course rubber and tin prices are rather more volatile than those of Malaya's other exports, and this affects the proportion from year to year. As Malaya's total exports to this area were just over one-sixth of its total exports to all countries, it is apparent that the remaining items of trade —comprising only about one-fifth of this trade, or one-thirtieth of the total—cannot be of very great significance. They amounted in all to about $M 125 million. Nearly two-thirds of this consisted of three groups of products—vegetable oils, coffee, and pepper, of which only the first was mainly produced in Malaya, the other two being entrepôt trade items.

The principal vegetable oil products included in the trade classification are coconut oil and palm oil, but there is also some export of copra and oil palm kernels. Total Malayan exports of these four products in 1956 were valued at $M 135 million. Imports of coconut and palm oil products, mainly for processing and re-export, during the same year were just under $M 50 million, so that about $M 85 million represented production, or value added in Malaya. About two-fifths of the coconut products and one-eighth of the oil palm products went in 1956 to the Common Market area, a total of $M 39 million (including copra and palm kernels), more than half of this total going to The Netherlands.

In comparison with the main items of Malaya's trade this is not an important item, yet in considering the impact of the Common Market and the Free Trade Area on the Federation of Malaya this is much the most important item to consider. One reason for this is simply that it is the most important single item by value. A second is that the rate of duty is not uniform within the Common Market at present and is open to negotiation between the countries concerned. A third is that in these products Malaya has important rivals in the French and Belgian colonies which will have free access into the Common Market. In addition, copra is an important smallholders' crop, palm oil is one of the growing points of Malayan agriculture, and the manufacture of vegetable oils in Malaya itself is a basis for some local industry.

Coffee and pepper are products entering into the entrepôt trade of Singapore and also of Penang, and both are likely to be affected, in ways not at present clearly predictable, by the Common Market policies, and perhaps also by the Free Trade Area. Total exports of these two products in 1956 to the Common Market area were valued at just over $M 50 million, or about 1¼ per cent of Malaya's total trade, but virtually none of this was produced in Malaya. Diversion of this trade elsewhere would therefore represent a much smaller loss to Malaya than to the producing countries, but in relation to the entrepôt trade of the two great ports it is certainly worthy of consideration.

Coffee is imported mainly from Sumatra, but also from Java and Bali.[7] It is exported to many countries, but a fairly high proportion (nearly three quarters in 1956) goes to the Common Market, principally Italy.[8] Denmark and the United Kingdom also import some, but Malaya's total exports of coffee to Free Trade Area countries outside the Common Market come to less than 10 per cent of total coffee exports. Insofar as the Free Trade Area negotiations are of any importance to this trade, it can only be through their effect on trade with the Common Market.

While concessions are made in the Rome treaty for imports of coffee into Italy and Belgium, these are to be only temporary, allowing these countries imports of coffee at their existing rates of duty on a

[7] Statistics in the text are based on the country summaries, and in some instances the detailed figures for commodities by country, in *Malayan Statistics: External Trade of Malaya, 1956* (Singapore: Register of Malayan Statistics, 1957).

[8] Imports to Italy were abnormally high in 1956; the proportion going to the Common Market is also commonly lower than three-quarters.

diminishing proportion of their current imports. It seems virtually certain that there will be diversion of trade to more expensive sources within the tropical dependencies of the Common Market. The main sufferer will be Indonesia, but Singapore's trade will clearly be adversely affected.

Pepper is imported mainly into Singapore, from Sarawak and Indonesia, and it is exported to many different markets. The Common Market area (excluding Morocco) takes slightly less than a quarter, the United Kingdom and the remainder of the Free Trade Area about the same, and the United States and Canada very slightly less. The remainder of the trade is scattered among many small markets, including substantial shipments to French Morocco. It will be seen, therefore, that the arrangements concerning pepper in the Common Market and Free Trade Area will affect nearly half of Malaya's trade in pepper, and these will therefore be of some concern to Singapore.

Pepper is to be treated as one of the agricultural products for which a common agricultural policy, including import stabilization in the interest of the agriculture of members of the European Economic Community, is to be worked out. About a quarter of the trade in pepper will be affected by the policy adopted, and a further quarter would be affected by any extension of the Free Trade Area to include agricultural products.

In their development plans for the future both the Federation of Malaya and Singapore have adopt-

ed policies which may be affected in some measure by
the establishment of a Common Market and the proposals for a Free Trade Area. The Federation's
chief emphasis is on diversification of agriculture,[9] on
attracting some of the processing and finishing industries from Singapore and elsewhere,[10] and on greater
self-sufficiency in food.[11] It is important to the
prosperity of Malaya that the diversification of agriculture should involve the development of other
crops for world markets, and should not be too much
directed into self-sufficiency in foodstuffs; and also
that its plans for industrialization should not lead to
too much conflict with Singapore, and a consequent
excessive disintegration of the present integrated
economy.

Apart from expansion of the export of vegetable
oils, preferably processed in Malaya, there are prospects of expanded sales of cocoa, canned pineapples
and other fruit, and the addition of Malayan coffee
and pepper to the varieties imported for re-export.
Negotiations not yet completed may appreciably affect
the development of important markets for all these
products. Cocoa is one of the products listed for
subsequent negotiation on rates of duty. If the
rate is high, with substantial preference for the

[9] International Bank for Reconstruction and Development,
op. cit., pp. 42-52, 189-212; Federation of Malaya, *Annual Report of the Department of Agriculture 1955* (Kuala Lumpur:
Government Printer, 1956), pp. 1-3, 78-87.
[10] Federation of Malaya, *Industrial Development Working
Party, Report* (Kuala Lumpur: Government Printer, 1957), pp.
18-25.
[11] Federation of Malaya, *Report on Economic Planning* (Kuala Lumpur: Government Printer, 1957), p. 4.

overseas territories of Common Market countries, one important potential market might well be closed to Malaya. It is also possible, though perhaps unlikely, that even the United Kingdom market would be affected indirectly through difficulties over the "origin" of chocolate products: for example, restrictions might be imposed on all new sources of imported cocoa into the United Kingdom as a condition of allowing British chocolate free access to the Free Trade Area, if a high rate of duty in the Common Market gave marked advantages to British producers.

Canned pineapples are already a fairly important Malayan industry, but a very high proportion goes to the United Kingdom. The other principal market is West Germany. This is a market that has developed fairly recently, and much will depend on what happens in the negotiations over agricultural policy in the Common Market, and over the role of agricultural products in the Free Trade Area. There is probably no serious immediate danger of competition in canned pineapples themselves from within the Common Market's overseas territories. Competition at a later stage is more than possible; but in the near future there may be diversion to other canned or preserved fruits. A restrictive agricultural policy might also hamper the growth of a canning industry for other Malayan fruits and vegetables.

An even more serious danger here is that negotiations over agriculture in the Free Trade Area might lead to modifications in the freedom of the United Kingdom market,[12] which would be much more serious for the pineapple industry and for prospects in other canned fruit and vegetables.

The impact of the Common Market and Free Trade Area on industrialization in Malaya is more indirect and indefinite. Like Hong Kong, Singapore will try to encourage industrialization mainly for Asian markets, related to its existing pattern of entrepôt trade; but opportunities may well open up for industries using local materials for export overseas; rubber, resins, spices, rattans, or other Straits produce. If the Common Market pursues a generally liberal policy toward imports of this kind the effect would be beneficial to Singapore directly, and indirectly also to the Federation; for any expansion in Singapore's external trade will diminish the risk of competition between Singapore and the Federation in the processing of rubber, timber, vegetable oils, and the like, which might advantageously be transferred to the Federation provided Singapore can maintain relatively high wages by development in other directions.

In some degree the addition of the Free Trade Area to the Common Market would strengthen those forces within the Common Market itself which favor a more liberal approach to trade with outside countries. But insofar as it failed to do this, the Free Trade Area would necessarily impose on the United Kingdom a policy of some restriction on the

[12] United Kingdom Council of the European Movement, *Agriculture and the Free Trade Area* (London, 1957).

import content of its exports. Anything which diminished the openness of the United Kingdom market to either manufactured goods or mixed goods based on entrepôt trade would be damaging to Malaya.

So far, opinion in Malaya has been very little concerned about either the Common Market or the Free Trade Area. There are at least three good explanations for this. First, Malaya is a small country, with relatively limited numbers of specialists, and during the last two years has been heavily preoccupied not only with political problems of independence but with associated economic problems; new central banking institutions, new tariff arrangements, and a largely new specialist service for its foreign affairs and international trade. The new relations between the Federation and Singapore naturally look much more important than arrangements for a Common Market in Europe.

The business structure in Malaya is also, in general, based more on rapid adaptation to short-run developments than on very long views. An economy making its way through the enormous price fluctuations of rubber and tin, and the uncertainties of emergent Asian economic nationalism all around it, has less occasion than more developed economies to look far into the future.

The direct effects of the Common Market and Free Trade Area, though they may ultimately be of some importance, do not affect Malaya's main products, and most of them are likely to be delayed several years, and to depend on negotiations which the

United Kingdom may be able to influence substantially but which Malaya can hardly affect. Not unnaturally, in the year of attaining independence, these are not negotiations that loom very large on Malaya's horizon.

Chambers of Commerce have barely referred to the European Common Market or the Free Trade Area, and the Malayan press has virtually neglected to comment. Almost the only political comment was in an interview by Dr. Ismail bin Dato Abdul Rahman, Permanent Delegate to the United Nations, in *Far East Trade*, August, 1957,[13] supporting the movement for European economic integration on the ground that it would expand income.

This indirect effect on the market for rubber and tin may well be the most important effect for Malaya. How important it will be depends on how much the income of Europe as a whole will benefit. Probably American influence has led to some exaggeration of the economic, as distinct from the political, advantages that are likely to accrue from this integration; but if even a moderate increase in income results, rubber and tin may benefit substantially, since both are products highly responsive to changes in the level of income.

It is difficult to forecast whether these indirect effects would be strengthened or weakened by the association with the Common Market of a wider Free Trade Area including the United Kingdom.

[13] "Shaping the Future," Special Interview with Dr. Ismail bin Dato Abdul Rahman, *Far East Trade*, XII (August, 1957), 170. Since the above was written the European Free Trade Area has been briefly discussed at the ECAFE Meeting in Kuala Lumpur, March, 1958.

On the one hand, if integration raises the average level of income in Europe, a wider integration would presumably raise it more. On the other, it is probable that for historical reasons British products use rather higher proportions of tin and natural rubber than corresponding European ones. Insofar as this is true, any gain by European products at the expense of British ones within the Free Trade Area might lead to some indirect substitution of synthetic for natural rubber or of tin substitutes for tin.[14] Superficially it seems unlikely that this would offset any expansive effect of increased prosperity.

We have already seen that the direct effect of the Common Market (taken by itself) on the minor items of Malaya's trade will depend mainly on negotiations which have yet to take place concerning agricultural policy and duties on vegetable oils. The effect of the association of the Free Trade Area with the Common Market will depend on a balance between two influences. The addition of the Free Trade Area may influence the Common Market in favor of a more liberal policy toward external trade and less discrimination in favor of the Common Market's own overseas territories; but it may also influence the United Kingdom towards a more controlled market for agricultural products.

[14] It has been pointed out to me by Sir Sydney Caine that this indirect substitution, to Malaya's disadvantage, is likely to occur in some measure as a result of the establishment of the Common Market, through preferences on industrial goods, so partially offsetting the advantages mentioned in the previous paragraph. It is, of course, uncertain how competition would develop in the Free Trade Area, and whether this would aggravate or reduce the disadvantage of Malaya.

If the United Kingdom makes concessions in the direction of a common agricultural policy for the sake of bringing the Free Trade Area into being, there is some danger that it will have to make concessions in respect of tropical products so as to protect, on the one hand, the United Kingdom farming interest, and on the other the preferences to Canada and Australasia. Such concessions would, of course, have to be paid for by the loss of some preferences for United Kingdom manufactures in tropical markets. But if this occurred, the balance of advantage on the Free Trade Area would probably be against Malaya, and the political effect would necessarily be damaging.

This brings us to certain fundamental attitudes on politico-economic questions which, in the absence of specific comment on the Common Market and Free Trade Area, will serve to illustrate Malaya's position.

First, Malaya is one of the newly independent Asian countries and shares with the rest of the Afro-Asian group an acute awareness of relative poverty and a belief that this is a result of colonial rule which has helped the countries of the West to grow rich. Though Malaya itself is fairly prosperous by Asian standards, it is by no means satisfied with its present absolute or relative position. Malayans, like other former colonial peoples, tend to believe that the developed countries have a moral obligation to help them to improve their economic standards, relatively as well as absolutely, as an act not of charity but of justice.

They are, therefore, likely to view with favor the provision of investment funds for the overseas territories of the Common Market, combined with special provisions for these territories to impose tariffs to foster their own development, and at the same time secure free access to the European market. They may, however, be suspicious of the political implications of an apparently permanent economic union in which the nature of the association is laid down by the European powers.

The European view, implied in the Rome Treaty and in the British practice of discontinuing Colonial Development and Welfare Fund assistance on the attainment of independence, appears to be that political independence logically implies an absence of external economic assistance. But it is important to understand, even if one does not accept, the Asian and African view, which is, broadly, that a changing balance of power and increasing influence of international public opinion are leading to correction of both political and economic injustices that arose as a result of the industrial revolution. On this view both political independence and economic aid in development are results of the same process, and there is certainly no logical contradiction between them.

Another basic politico-economic attitude in Malaya is its comparative distrust of autarky and willingness to accept a regime of international specialization. This is, of course, more marked in Singapore, the great entrepôt port of Asia, than in the Federation. But even the Federation has a fairly clear recognition that its prosperity depends on a high degree of specialization. Like other trading countries, it wishes to cut down its dependence on foreign food supplies below the level that a free market would dictate; and it is also anxious to diversify its economy somewhat, mainly to lessen its dependence on two raw materials which both happen to suffer extreme fluctuations in price. But its development plans do not indicate a passion for heavy industries or acute sensitiveness to its dependence on foreign trade.

This will certainly make it easier for Malaya to cope with its rapid increase of population. But it will also keep Malaya interested in a flexible international economy. If the Common Market is a step in the direction of freer international trade, and particularly if the Free Trade Area results in extending to others some of the unilateral privileges to be enjoyed by the overseas territories of the Common Market, it is likely to find support in Malaya.

It must be hoped, however, that such privileges will be related, not to political dependency, but to level of development. Like the other Asian and African members of the Commonwealth, Malaya is likely to maintain its position in the Commonwealth, not mainly for defense reasons, but because it provides a bridge of common institutions across the gulf in thinking which divides the recently emancipated colonial territories from the economically developed countries of the West.

This is what the Commonwealth means to Asia, and this would appear to suggest one appropriate role for the United Kingdom in the Free Trade Area negotiations. In any supranational organization the fact must be faced that the ideological conditions do not yet exist for strong international institutions, and it is therefore important to avoid intermediate institutions which will emphasize the more troublesome existing divisions. The Common Market could become an exclusive club, merely protecting the high standard of living of the developed European countries and of a few continuing dependencies. Extension to a Free Trade Area should not simply widen the membership and perhaps bring in a few more dependencies.

Progress along these lines would be frustrated from the start. Malaya's own position, with virtually a common economy shared between an independent country on the one hand and on the other a city state, dependent in foreign policy but not in trade, draws attention to the difficulty.

It may be mentioned in passing that if the United Kingdom negotiated special Free Trade Area terms for its own manufactures made from Commonwealth raw materials, this would seriously injure Singapore's vital entrepôt trade in rubber, which is based on mixed imports from the Federation, Borneo, and Indonesia.

Within the Commonwealth, aid can find models either in the Colombo Plan, where development and need are the criteria, or in the Colonial Development and Welfare Fund, which is linked to colonial status. The Common Market, in addition to providing for intergovernmental aid, has made a useful start in tariff provisions which favor certain underdeveloped countries without diminishing their power to protect their own developing industries. It is to be hoped that the United Kingdom will use its influence during the development of the Common Market into a Free Trade Area to foster a policy on agriculture and raw materials tariffs which will be generous to underdeveloped countries as such, on the basis not of dependency but of need in the flexible spirit of the Colombo Plan.

5

The Determinants of Economic Development

In recent years increasing attention has been devoted by economists to the problem of promoting economic growth in the so-called "underdeveloped areas of the world." Probably the quest for useful generalizations as a guide to policy in this field is a fruitful one; and a number of interesting suggestions about capital formation, adaptation of technologies, and the like have been made.[1] Neverthe-

[1] There is already an extensive literature in this field. A good survey of the field is C. Wolf and C. S. Sufrin, *Capital Formation and Foreign Investment in Underdeveloped Areas* (Syracuse: Syracuse University Press, 1955). There is also an admirable bibliography relevant to Southeast Asia in Sumitro Djojohadikusumo, *Ekonomi Pembangunan* (Djakarta: P. T. Pembangunan, 1955), pp. 352-362. Probably the standard general works on the subject are W. A. Lewis, *The Theory of Economic Growth* (London: Allen and Unwin, 1955), and Norman S. Buchanan and Howard S. Ellis, *Approaches to Economic Development* (New York: Twentieth Century Fund, 1955). See also United Nations, *Measures for the Development of Underdeveloped Countries,* a report prepared by a group of experts appointed by the Secretary-General, United Nations (New York: Department of Economic Affairs, 1951). This broad factorial approach has been strongly criticized, e.g., by S. H. Frankel in *Some Aspects of International Economic Development of Under-*

less, it must be emphasized that the general term "underdeveloped areas" covers a large part of the world and that the different underdeveloped countries differ from one another in a number of respects which are distinctly relevant to the problem of promoting economic development. This means in the first instance that economic development will be a different problem in each different country and that the economy of the country must be studied in detail if useful economic advice is to be given. So much is obvious. But because of the comparative scarcity of economists with detailed knowledge of each of these countries, we must try to secure some economies of scale in the application of economics, and try to indicate the general lines on which fundamental economic theory can be adapted to certain broadly measurable characteristics of different economies.

---

developed Territories (Princeton: Department of Economics and Social Institutions, Princeton University, 1952; also reprinted by Oxford University, Institute of Colonial Studies, Reprint series No. 5), and in the review of the above United Nations publication by P. T. Bauer in the *Economic Journal*, LXIII (March, 1953), 210-222. Cf. also S. H. Frankel, *The Economic Impact on Underdeveloped Societies* (Oxford: B. Blackwell, 1953). More specialized approaches to the problem of promoting economic development include historical and anthropological analyses of the conditions for the development of enterprise, e.g., W. W. Rostow, *The Process of Economic Growth* (Oxford: Clarendon Press, 1953), C. S. Belshaw, *In Search of Wealth*, American Anthropological Association Memoir No. 80, February, 1955; studies of investment requirements and investment criteria, e.g., the M. I. T. Center for International Studies Symposium on "Investment Criteria and Economic Growth," 1956, and a considerable number of United Nations publications, especially by ECLA and ECAFE; and more technical economic studies of the implications of growth, e.g., Joan Robinson, *The Accumulation of Capital* (London: Macmillan, 1956).

The present chapter is an attempt to classify some of the respects in which various underdeveloped economies may differ in characteristics relevant to the problems of promoting economic development. It attempts also to give some preliminary indications of how these differences can be taken into account.

A preliminary enumeration of the relevant determinants that will be considered is as follows:

1. The degree of isolation of the economy.

2. The present availability and the present rate of change of the different broad factors of production including:

    (a) Land and exploitable mineral resources.

    (b) Capital.

    (c) Enterprise and management skills.

    (d) Unskilled labor and facilities for training skills.

3. Social values bearing on the diffusion of enterprise and skill, the acceptance of innovations, and the growth of large-scale economic institutions.

4. Strength or weakness of the administration, in relation to the territories to be covered and the economic tasks to be performed, and the basic attitudes of the population toward the role of the state in economic life.

Some consideration is also given to the possibilities of influencing economic development if it is heavily dependent on international trade. It is well known that the Southeast Asian economies depend very much on a few major exports, such as copra, rice, rubber, sugar, tea, and tin.

Closed economies are often considered much more manipulable in promoting development than open ones (especially the so-called colonial economies). But here much depends on the type of national or international action we are considering. If we are taking the point of view of the government of the country concerned, an open economy is probably in general rather less manipulable than a closed one because large-scale dependence on foreign markets, foreign specialists or entrepreneurs, and a continual flow of foreign investment imposes important limitations on a government's economic policy. These limitations may go rather further than is at first apparent because of possibilities of substitution between products or factors which are under the influence of foreign countries and products or factors which are not. For example, a government's policy in control of monopolies may be seriously handicapped because drastic control of certain foreign monopolies might have serious consequences for its economy, whilst it may be politically or even economically difficult to distinguish between local and foreign firms in legislative and administrative action.

But though a closed economy may be more manipulable in this sense, it may be less manipulable by international action if we are considering how best to raise the standard of living of underdeveloped countries by international action. It would clearly be easier to give assistance to a country if it already has contacts with the remainder of the world than if it has not. For example, countries which wished to foster its development could give tariff preferences to its products, could introduce new and more far-reaching servicing arrangements in existing import agencies, and could in many cases give assistance through an existing group of people resident in the country. Similarly, strictly international action could offer assistance through monetary or trade channels by simply modifying existing trade practices. An example of national assistance being facilitated by extensive international contacts is postwar American assistance to the Philippines; while some of the difficulties of United Nations assistance to Korea have been due to lack of existing trade connections, except those with Japan and China, which were politically unacceptable to an independent South Korea.

Up to the present, however, there has been rather a lack of organized international assistance to the more open economies by indirect means. It would appear, for example, that concessions granted to underdeveloped countries by waiving the general rules of the International Monetary Fund or the General Agreement on Tariffs and Trade have been made reluctantly and with no very obvious intention of using these international instruments to accelerate the relative rate of development of the less developed countries. This is especially unfortunate because it means that international aid tends to operate in favor of the autarkic tendencies that are already strongly accentuated by national feeling in underdeveloped countries. Though these autarkic tendencies are certainly strong in underdeveloped countries, there are important elements which operate against this trend.

If an economy has extensive foreign relations, it will often be possible to convert it into a more closed economy only at very considerable cost. If the climate of international opinion is favorable, it may well pay a country better to retain its open character and rely on international diplomacy to create favorable conditions for international promotion of development. Several countries of Asia appear to be moving in the direction of exploiting their bargaining position in this way rather than attempting to move towards greater self-sufficiency. If it were possible for the countries of this region to secure more economic co-operation with one another, they might be able to move very much further in this direction.

This brings out a further point that is most relevant to comparisons between the economies of different countries, namely, the absolute size of the country concerned. It is natural that small and weak countries should try to improve their position by imitating successful achievements of larger and stronger countries. It is, however, usually fallacious to assume that such imitations will necessarily bring success. A small country may not be able to achieve many of the economies of scale which are so important a feature of industrialization. Therefore, in order to insure a rapid rise in the standard of living it is often necessary to specialize and to overcome the danger of economic dependence by cultivating a wider range of economic relationships rather than by withdrawing toward a closed economy.

Whether the economy is an open or a closed one, it will be necessary in planning economic development to be constantly aware of the special characteristics of the economy, particularly in its supplies of the main factors of production. With a relatively closed economy, it will be necessary to supply a wider range of products and therefore to modify techniques imported from overseas more than in a relatively open economy. International trade is in part a substitute for modification of techniques, for with international trade a country can specialize in those products in which its relative advantages are greatest, and it will often happen that in these it suffers less disadvantage as a result of its low level of development and therefore needs less modification of techniques. This is not, of course, always the situation. Malaya's abundant supplies of tin have for many years given it an advantage in specializing on this product, but the different characteristics of labor, the availability of water power, and the frequency of alluvial deposits have made it profitable to develop different techniques in Malaya from those that prevail elsewhere. Nevertheless, it will generally be true that a relatively open economy will specialize in products in which its relative disadvantage in factors of production is less and will not therefore need so drastic a modification of techniques.

To decide on the appropriate techniques to encourage and the appropriate economic institutions to develop, we need to consider more fully the supplies of the basic factors of production.

We may begin with the land and natural resources available in any given economy. The most important fact to bear in mind about land in most of the countries of Southeast Asia is that it is a resource of which large proportions are likely to remain unused for lack of complementary resources. The concept of scarcity applies to particular kinds of land and in some areas, of which Singapore is one, it may apply to land as a whole. Generally, however, the land is of very variable quality, and the extent to which it is utilized depends on the availability of complementary resources. Capital must be expended on irrigation systems and on transport routes to open up particular tracts of country, and because this capital is a scarce resource with alternative uses, only those parts of the land where the amount to be invested is relatively small have so far been used in most of the areas of Southeast Asia.

In some respects this is true of places like Java, South China, and Japan where the land is already very heavily used, but here the development of new land is probably only marginal. Elsewhere in Southeast Asia, for some time to come the development of new land resources is primarily a matter of available capital. In some instances, however, the capital required includes costs of transport and perhaps even inducements to promote migration of population from crowded to less crowded areas.

The countries of the region do, however, differ

appreciably in the availability of additional land which is usable without greater capital cost than is normally expended on existing land in use. In India and Ceylon considerable additional expenditures on irrigation are necessary to develop additional land. In Indonesia the main problem is one of inducing surplus population to move from one part of the territory to others, and this is a major capital expenditure, comparable with that which other countries need to incur for irrigation. In most of the countries of Southeast Asia, however, additional land is available subject to the solving of political difficulties and the opening up of transport. This also is a capital cost but not appreciably greater than the capital cost incurred already in developing existing land.

We may turn therefore to the problem of capital formation in Southeast Asia. One important source of capital is the mineral resources available in the countries of the region. Generally the discovery of some mineral of international demand within the territory of a country leads to a substantial but temporary additional income accruing in that country, and it is generally considered to be desirable that part of this should be invested in capital construction so that the high income secured can be continued. This may be done if the land is owned by local inhabitants and a proportion of the royalties earned is put into a depreciation reserve which is locally invested or invested in overseas assets.[2] Where the land is government land, royalties can be used for development

[2] In Malaya, of course, such royalties are negligible, and export duties are levied instead.

projects or paid into reserves.[3] Frequently, however, the discovery of these resources has in fact been carried out by foreign firms, and extraction has been treated simply as a source of revenue with depreciation provision in foreign countries. In some of the British territories, and particularly in Malaya, fairly substantial capital works have been constructed out of revenue which was directly or indirectly derived from the consumption of wasting natural resources. There has, however, been relatively little attempt to treat such resources as wasting assets of the country concerned.

In the main, capital formation is the result of a surplus of income over consumption during a fairly prolonged period. It must be emphasized, however, that this income is not normally limited to income in the sense in which that term is used by the Internal Revenue authorities. Assets must, of course, be constructed by organizing factors of production to make them. But a substantial part of capital formation in underdeveloped areas consists in raising the value of such assets by creating successful and continuing businesses to use them. The value of the assets in underdeveloped countries held by overseas shareholders commonly includes several different layers of capital gains from the time of the initial construction of the physical capital.[4]

[3] Much of the early development of Malaya, especially its transport system, was financed from tin revenues. See Sir Lewis L. Fermor, *Report upon the Mining Industry of Malaya* (Kuala Lumpur: Government Printer, 1943).

[4] For examples in rubber and tin, see D. M. Figart, *The Plantation Rubber Industry in the Middle East* (prepared as part

If the stock of capital is to be increased, it is necessary both to use existing factors of production for the construction of new assets and to insure that consumption is sufficiently restricted so that such use of factors of production will generate no inflationary pressure.[5]

The creation of the assets is at least as important a part of capital formation as the restriction of consumption. Within any underdeveloped country restriction of consumption by itself can do positive harm by aggravating local unemployment. No doubt the chief source of this unemployment is the lack of complementary resources, but if there is a falling off in consumption, this will not in itself help to stimulate capital formation in an underdeveloped country any more than in a more developed one. Indeed, the effect is likely to be even more harmful because factors are probably less mobile.

In this respect attention should be drawn to Frankel's emphasis on the misleading character of aggregate estimates of capital and the great importance of concrete projects of capital construction.[6] Frankel, however, appears to go further than is justifiable in condemning the usefulness of attempting to generate international willingness to transfer very

---

of the survey of essential raw materials authorized by the Sixty-seventh Congress), U. S. Bureau of Foreign and Domestic Commerce, Department of Commerce, Trade Promotion Series no. 2 (Washington: Government Printing Office, 1925), and J. K. Eastham, "Rationalisation in the Tin Industry," *Review of Economic Studies*, IV (1936), 13-32.

[5] Joan Robinson, *op. cit.*, pp. 83 ff.

[6] S. H. Frankel, *Some Aspects of International Economic Development of Underdeveloped Territories*, pp. 21-22.

large sums of capital to underdeveloped countries with the minimum possible obligation to repay or even to pay interest or profits.

It is not generally suggested that these large international transfers should be direct gifts of foreign exchange for underdeveloped countries to invest themselves in interest-earning assets. They can take the form of backing for investment while at the same time relieving some of the balance of payments difficulties of an undeveloped country, or they can take the form of direct grants, as suggested by the United Nations experts commission,[7] for assisting educational or medical expenditures which will promote economic growth indirectly.

It is common for underdeveloped countries to lack the right combination of capital resources and entrepreneurial skill. Where either the home government or a foreign government can make public funds available, it will then be necessary to use them in one of two ways. One way is to direct them into those lines where no great amount of enterprise is needed and where what is required can be provided by the government itself. Examples are the manufacture of cement or fertilizers, which have been increasingly undertaken in recent years by the governments of underdeveloped countries. The alternative is to concentrate on lines in which enterprise is already available but is hampered by lack of capital. Development of fisheries is one example and the extension of road transport services is another.

[7] United Nations, *Measures for the Development of Underdeveloped Countries.*

Generally, this latter type of assistance to development implies greater inventiveness in devising new institutional forms than the former type. Local enterprise may take forms which do not lend themselves easily to development by outside capital. Western forms of accounting, pledging of assets, etc., will often be unfamiliar and if capital is supplied unintelligently, the result may be merely to build up monopolies in the hands of a few people who have some understanding of these techniques. A good deal of investigation is needed to make it possible for the ordinary competent fishermen to acquire a powered boat or for a group of small farmers to acquire the services of tractors and other mechanical aids.

Not enough is known as yet about the conditions in which enterprise grows, and we should certainly not take too seriously the popular propaganda which suggests that the chief requirement is low taxation and firm guarantees against possible nationalization. It is almost certain that these will do virtually nothing to stimulate the growth of a class of entrepreneurs, though it must be conceded that they may do something in attracting foreign entrepreneurs to one country rather than another. If taxation remains low, it will not be possible to develop a high level of technical education or to do much to build up the social overheads such as transport or power which are necessary if local enterprise is to flourish. Nor will guarantees against nationalization as such count for very much unless the government is firmly controlled by the existing business interest; and such control is hardly consistent with a flexible and progressive economy. It is much more important that the proceeds of taxation should be used directly or indirectly for development, and that any nationalization should be part of a predictable pattern of economic policy.

Keynes has emphasized that it is uncertainty, rather than high predictable risks, which is hampering to business confidence. And though businessmen would probably not support a party with a program of high taxation and systematic nationalization of a certain range of industries, they might well show more constructive activity under a government with a consistent policy of economic development than under a government which tried to woo business by general tax concessions and guarantees, and to woo the electors by general nationalistic catch-words.

It is important that the countries of Asia, and underdeveloped countries generally, should make up their minds that if they need a high level of taxation for securing a rapid rate of growth, and if they need to have some industries under national ownership as part of their essential economic planning, they should not compete with one another in throwing these advantages away for the sake of attracting the marginal international capitalist. In certain cases foreign capital may be badly needed, and it may be practicable to allow generous tax concessions and guarantees against nationalization in order to attract this capital. But it is far more important to attempt to build up local enterprise and local capital formation than to create a generally favorable investment climate for the international capitalist.

Although high taxation as such is not necessarily a deterrent to capital formation, it is of some importance to design taxation in such a way as to encourage reinvestment of profits, particularly by small firms, since this leads to a more rapid growth of a local entrepreneurial class. There is obviously less advantage in stimulating reinvestment by large firms, and what is important is to create adequate local institutions which will make it more convenient for such firms to spread their risks by reinvesting profits in other local industries, since an active capital market will make it easier for local entrepreneurs to expand their business once they begin to achieve success. Something may be done by giving inducements to large firms to reinvest in local industries rather than abroad, but it is not easy to go very far in this direction without interfering with the right to remit reasonable profits overseas, which usually has to be conceded to attract foreign capital.

Probably too little attention has been paid by underdeveloped countries to training in the techniques of accountancy and business management. There is probably adequate appreciation of the fact that such training is productive, but not enough appreciation of the need to adapt it to local methods of doing business in such a way that it can become a constructive force for growth. This appears to be a most fruitful field for sociological research, since what is required is probably not the conversion of Chinese or Thai or

Indian firms into firms on the European model but rather a more sophisticated and accurate system of recording and institutionalizing of their own business forms.

It is obviously not sensible to treat the Chinese tontine system as an illegal form of capital formation or to encourage the transformation of Chinese partnerships into limited companies. Very possibly some cross-fertilization could take place between these established business forms and some of the forms that have facilitated such enormous concentration of capital in the West. New research in these fields may well develop forms of technical training that would strengthen the growth of local enterprise in many of the Southeast Asian countries.

Rapid population growth creates additional needs for capital formation. The quantity of capital per head may not be a very precise concept,[8] but it is certainly not wholly fallacious to suggest that the national capital must in some sense increase at a similar percentage rate to the population if the capital per head is not to fall; and this increase is clearly greater the greater is the growth of the population. Many of the countries of Southeast Asia have populations increasing at about 3 per cent per annum, and where this has not yet been reached, the rate of

---

[8] Robinson, *op. cit.*, especially chap. ii, for discussion of the difficulties of definition here. Some of the difficulties appear to be aggravated by the particular macro-economic approach adopted, partial solutions having been worked out by J. R. Hicks, *Value and Capital* (2nd ed., Oxford: Clarendon Press, 1946), Book IV, and F. A. von Hayek, *Pure Theory of Capital* (London: Routledge and Kegan Paul, 1950), chap. xv, under a different and equally consistent approach.

growth is rapidly approaching this figure. This implies that about 10 per cent of the national income must be devoted to net capital formation if these economies are not to grow poorer in capital equipment per head than they were before (assuming that the ratio of capital to income at the margin is about 3:1).

This generalization must be accepted with some caution since the expansion of capital at the same rate as population is not an absolutely necessary condition of the maintenance of income per head. It is possible for improved technical knowledge to offset a declining supply of capital per head; though improved technical knowledge means more training, and training problems are themselves seriously aggravated by a rapid rate of population growth. Probably agricultural extension work is the most hopeful of all lines of investment at present. It is possible in some countries for economies of scale to be important in capital supply so that it is not necessary to build twice as many power stations or dams when the population doubles. Here again these economies of scale do not appear likely to be important except possibly in countries like Sarawak or North Borneo, where population is very sparse indeed. In overpopulated countries even a proportional increase in capital would not be sufficient because scarcity of land would make it necessary to construct new capital as a substitute for land, for example, in taking population off the soil by industrialization.

It is sometimes argued that a high rate of population growth itself contributes to capital formation. On the one hand, it can be claimed than an expanding population makes it possible to develop all kinds of new capital, without competing with existing capital, so that the risk of capital loss is reduced and investment incentives are therefore strengthened; on the other hand, it can be claimed that the greatest incentive to saving is provision for one's children, and therefore more children per head will mean more savings.

We need waste little time on the second argument; it is fallacious to assume that the incentive to save operates with maximum intensity when the number of children is largest; and we must consider the ability to save as well as the incentive to do so. Beyond a certain point the task of adequate provision is felt to be hopeless, and people are content to live from hand to mouth. There is abundant evidence all over the world that the desire to raise the economic status of one's children becomes a more effective force when a moderate degree of saving can achieve really significant improvement.

It is probably true that capital formation is less risky in an expanding economy, and this would be an important argument against working for a stationary population in any country in which land was not seriously scarce; but it seems highly improbable that even a large reduction in the risks of investment would offset the drain on capital of a population increase of 3 per cent.

The prospect for a rise in standards of living

based on capital formation therefore appears somewhat gloomy in underdeveloped countries, and it is important that people's expectations should not be unduly raised. In particular it needs to be stressed that a government is not necessarily investing capital unintelligently and bungling its economic planning if large and obvious capital projects fail to raise the standard of living rapidly. Most of the underdeveloped countries of the world need to run very fast in capital formation if they are to stay where they are, and our problem is not merely one of achieving some narrowing of the gap between the wealthiest and the poorest countries but one of insuring that the poorest countries do not actually grow poorer.

It is perhaps insufficiently appreciated that the amount of international aid which is given at present falls very far short of the amount of redistributive taxation that is found in even a fairly unprogressive country in the modern world, and there would appear to be much stronger reasons to suppose that inequalities of income between countries are cumulative in effect than to suppose that they are cumulative within a given country. Only rather drastic redistributive taxation is sufficient in most individual countries to prevent the gap between the rich and the poor from increasing; but when we consider the comparisons between countries the problem is aggravated by differential rates of population growth which, for example, are much greater between Northwestern Europe and Southeast Asia than they have ever been between different classes in any one country.

It would therefore be unreasonable to expect that the gap in income between the richest and the poorest countries will be narrowed or even prevented from widening until political education has proceeded much further in the direction of free international transfers of resources. No doubt in due course and if there is no major war, the trend of political development will take us far enough for some narrowing of this gap to take place. But, however desirable it may be to encourage capital formation, we should not do it by holding out the hope of a very rapid improvement in the relative standard of living in any of the underdeveloped countries, when very substantial capital formation and capital transfer are essential to prevent a relative deterioration.

This brings us to the consideration of the role of the labor force in economic development. The rapid growth of population implies not merely a rapid rate of increase in the labor force but a change in the structure of the population so that the proportion of those of working age is relatively much less than in a stable population. The rate of growth has to be very high before the proportion of non-workers to workers is seriously affected in comparison with a more stable population because fewer old people must be weighed against more children; but where rates of 3 per cent or 4 per cent are reached the proportion of children who are not earning can become a relatively serious burden on the economy. Much more important, however, is the effect on educational standards.

If we compare a population increasing at $3\frac{1}{2}$ per cent with one which is stationary, the proportion of the population that will need to be employed as teachers to achieve a given level of education will be between three and four times as great in the former as in the latter. Moreover, since underdeveloped countries are almost invariably backward in education, the strain of providing this number of teachers is proportionately much more serious than in a developed country. This strain manifests itself in the form of either high earnings or low standards among teachers, and in either case the quality of education that can be purchased for a given cost is further reduced.

These facts add to the difficulty of developing improved techniques, at least by any of the normal methods of imitation of the practices of more developed countries. More developed countries base their provision of technicians on the fundamental structure of universal education and on selection according to ability. If universal primary education is sacrificed, the selection of enough technicians of ability becomes more difficult. These basic problems in the provision of technical personnel and their relation to the demographic structure appear to have been insufficiently appreciated, and they may well call for more radical modifications of Western methods of instituting development programs than would at first seem desirable.

Another factor that needs to be pointed out is the competition of new skills with traditional skills and the deliberate resistance that this competition may provoke. This is most obvious in the resistance to the competition of immigrants, but it is a force to be reckoned with in any attempt to improve levels of skill. Normally, building labor, for example, will not openly oppose the introduction of additional training to improve the standards of skill but will contrive indirect means of hampering a program which may render its own skill redundant. Nationalism is very commonly invoked to hamper the development of new skills, especially where this is done by importing foreign technicians as trainers.

Specialist skill has often in the past been introduced by importing labor from another economy in which this skill was relatively abundant. All over Southeast Asia there are groups of specialist workers who have been introduced to perform special functions for European capitalists and have established themselves as more or less separate minorities in the countries in which they have settled. There can be no question that the economies of Southeast Asia have developed more rapidly because of the possibility of importing these skills; but beyond a certain point the existence of these immigrants may be a barrier to further progress because they hamper the development of local training. If there is a local group of migrants from a foreign country which performs a given function in the economy but remains culturally separate, it will have a strong vested interest in preventing the training of local competitors and may well have the power to stop its taking place. This situation will not arise if the migrant group has no hope of continuing beyond a limited period.

Diffusion of a migrant's skill can be fairly rapid if the migrant is wholly absorbed, as usually has happened in North America, or if he is avowedly transient, as has happened in West Africa. The presence of migrants who are neither fully assimilated nor avowedly transient can be an important barrier to local training, as may be seen in East Africa, parts of South America, and some of the countries of Southeast Asia.

The consideration of the role of migrants and the diffusion of their skill necessarily brings us to a discussion of social values and their effect on economic activity. Migrants, and particularly refugees, have had a stimulating effect on economic growth in a great many countries both in Northwestern Europe, in the United States, and more recently in India and Hong Kong. This might be because people from economically superior countries are driven to another country and introduce progressive ideas there; but this is by no means always a full account of the situation. It may have been true in England or in the United States, though in neither case is this at all obvious. In India and Hong Kong there appear to be clear examples of migrants from less developed regions who have nevertheless introduced favorable conditions for economic development.

This would appear to suggest that the impulse to change is itself an important aspect of economic development. Possibly social values as such tend to have a conservative tendency in most societies, and the mere fact that they are subject to pressure and change makes for adaptability to the economic possibilities and hence for economic development. Moreover, migrants even from less developed regions are usually not a representative sample of the population but selected for adaptability by circumstances. For similar reasons economic development is often rapid in great ports where the meeting of different cultures leads to a greater fluidity of social values.

Economic progress appears to demand at least some willingness to work for economic progress. But it is interesting that the motive of desire for economic improvement as such has not been the dominant motive in many of the instances of most rapid development.[9] It appears to be true that the early capitalists in England valued wealth more as an indication of success in their vocation than for the benefits it would confer, and such success in their vocation was regarded as evidence of religious salvation. In both Japan and the Soviet Union an important motive of economic development has been the desire for national power or security.

There must indeed be a willingness to apply scientific knowledge to economic needs and to experiment and devise new techniques. These values appear to be essential; but the impulse to the enjoyment of wealth is in part a check on rapid capital formation, which is one of the requirements for rapid economic growth.

[9] Rostow, *op. cit.*, pp. 45-46, 104-108; Buchanan and Ellis, *op. cit.*, pp. 147-150, 175-212.

One of the social values which is worth mentioning at this point is the recognition of individuals as playing a specific role within an organization, and achieving success or failure according to their capacity to carry out the role efficiently. This implies a rather more impersonal attitude than is common in Asian cultures, yet it is probably a more widespread requirement in economic life than is generally recognized. It is obvious that some of the technical specializations that make modern business organizations so powerful require this kind of impersonality. It is difficult to see, however, how these specializations can fit into a form of business organization in which other personnel are not also playing a pre-assigned, and objectively defined, role.

Some comments may be made here also about the place of the state in promoting economic development, though the subject is too large for exhaustive treatment. Since we are discussing economic policy, we are mainly concerned with how legal and administrative action can bring about economic development. In other words, we are looking at it from the point of view of government or of the citizens or experts who bring some influence to bear on government. The promotion of economic development, however, can take the form either of trying to create suitable conditions for various private activities to take place or of undertaking economic activities directly through the apparatus of government control.

First, we may regard the choice of public or private enterprise as a choice influenced by the availability of scarce resources. It can be argued that in certain conditions the use of the state apparatus can economize resources, since an initiative taken by the government can be diffused through the whole chain of subordinates of the central government, so making use of an existing machine when any comparable initiative by two or three private individuals could not possibly have so great an impact. Where the progress involved is that of developing a system of communications or irrigation or of introducing some scheme for modifying agricultural practice, arguments of this kind are probably valid. The research can be done under government auspices and once the results are known and suitable techniques devised, it is probably easier for the government to mobilize the necessary resources. Where it is a question of operating factories for making chemicals or locomotives, the question of whether or not the government should do it essentially depends on which method is more efficient and productive. Generally, there would be advantages on both sides, and in either case it should be possible to retain some surplus, if a surplus is earned, for further development.

Some economy can be secured if development is in private hands because some of the training necessary for an official can be dispensed with, and this widens the possible fields of supply. Also it is probably true that the private employer has greater freedom of action and initiative because he is not tied down by precedent. On the whole it is unlikely that a private enterprise will take as little in salary, profit, and commissions as government servants would require in salary. An appreciable part of what it takes in profit may, however, be reinvested, so that from the point of view of economic development all that may be lost is some control over the direction of the development process. Moreover, it is very probable that the private employer who earns good profits will have intelligent ideas about other lines of development.

So far the argument appears to favor the encouragement of development in private hands. On the other hand, it is probable that governments can secure information from overseas and probably also borrow technicians more cheaply than private undertakings, and can do more about insuring that their knowledge will be diffused. Probably the main argument in favor of government planning in this sphere, if we leave strictly political arguments out of account, is that private employers cannot profitably undertake training on any considerable scale without training up potential rivals, while the government can integrate its training program with its industrialization program; and in processes involving a large range of new skills this may be a decisive factor.

When we pass on to consider possible administrative and legal pressures on business we need to take account of the nature of the administrative machine which the government commands, and the nature of the territory and population which it is administering. It should be obvious that control of the frontiers would be easier in, say, Pakistan than in Indonesia because of the nature of the terrain. Also some countries have a much more adequate supply of reliable and well trained officials than others. Either rapid transition from colonial rule or heavy inflation may lead to the growth of corruption and unreliability on a large scale. In some instances the framework of the state which has developed from local political origins is not well adapted to the task of economic control, perhaps because of a tradition of senior political officers undertaking economic operations for their own profit. Sometimes, on the other hand, a colonial administrative machine which is probably fairly well designed for a foreign trade economy, may be found to be far too narrow in scope when the role of government is rapidly expanding, particularly if large numbers of expatriates leave the service on transfer of power.

It would appear to be a matter of great importance to avoid trying to impose on the economy of any country controls which might be appropriate to other countries but are unlikely to be effective because of difficulties of terrain or overstraining of the administrative machine.

It is sometimes argued that if the administrative machine is weak, it is undesirable for it to waste its energies on operating economic undertakings of any kind. It is certainly undesirable for it to extend its functions unnecessarily; but it is probably a mistake to argue that it is always more economical in staff to control economic undertakings and secure their conformity to the national interest by over-all controls rather than by direct administration. If the structure of these organizations is reasonably efficient and the administrative machine is not, it may be more economical (provided the political conditions favor it) to effect a change in control at the top rather than attempt to pit the officials of the government against the skilled subordinates of a number of efficient companies. Relations with the oil industry in several Asian countries, for example, have shown that greater control of the contribution which an industry can make to the economy can be achieved by an agreed form of joint operation than by attempting to administer over-all controls of exchange or trade. The point to make is that the lack of trained staff to implement economic policies should be recognized and the degree of interference with free economic forces be reduced to what can actually be achieved with existing staff.

In any attempt to promote development, it will be necessary to watch the external relations of the national economy. These include both formal and diplomatic relations with foreign governments and direct economic relations with the world market. Some forms of development, particularly if they involve nationalization or rapid transfer of personnel, may involve political difficulties, but these are perhaps outside our scope. Frequently development involves balance of payments difficulties, partly because capital construction may have a higher import content than the consumption goods which it replaces and partly because the income elasticity of demand for imports may be greater than unity so that a rise in income itself leads to difficulties unless the development is specially orientated toward exports. In comparing different economies we must bear in mind that the restrictive effect of balance of payments difficulties may be much greater in some than in others.

The countries which are best off are those in which a few export products have either a rapidly expanding or a very elastic demand and in which the supply can be expanded provided sufficient capital can be invested in these exports. In the Southeast Asian area, however, most of the exports are subject to great fluctuations in prices and the different governments are therefore reluctant to base too much of their policy on increased export promotion. It is likely that in good years Malaya, and probably the Borneo territories also, could avoid balance-of-payments difficulties by devoting a high proportion of their development expenditure to expanding the rubber industry.[10] Few countries, however, would be disposed to go even as far as Malaya in putting their eggs into such an insecure basket.

A democratic government, which has no wish to exercise totalitarian control over an entire economy, can still influence economic development by several other devices than the establishment of public enterprises. It can influence prices directly, it can widen or narrow income differences, it can control the sup-

---

[10] See the comments in International Bank, *Report on the Economic Development of Malaya* (Singapore: Government Printer, 1955), pp. 11, 21, 34-41, 182-185.

plies of consumer goods and factors of production or ration those already in existence, and it can use the fiscal mechanism to affect prices and incomes or to influence economic activity indirectly. The price system operates most effectively in those parts of the economy where people are already sophisticated in a financial sense and ready to adjust their behavior in response to price differences. Where people will plant certain seed if the relation between the cost and the yield is markedly favorable, the government may be able to influence cultivation practices simply by selling certain types of seed at a heavily subsidized rate. Where the government owns extensive resources such as lands or forests, it can often influence economic activity by raising or depressing prices of products in such a way as to make various lines of activity which it wishes to promote more profitable.

In many underdeveloped economies, however, sharp modification of prices is more likely to lead to political reactions than to cause appropriate modifications of economic behavior. The price system operates as an effective inducement only when some rudimentary enterprise is already at work in the economy. There are, therefore, rather definite limits to the extent to which it can be used as an instrument for development where the main problem is the modification of an economy in which subsistence agriculture plays an important part.

In some respects the stimulation of economic development is similar to the mobilization of an economy for war; in others it is different. In war it might theoretically be possible to raise sufficient taxes to divert all the required resources into the making of munitions or even into the armed forces. In practice, however, the job is always done by some measure of compulsion assisted by inflation. In an underdeveloped economy, our problem is not the problem of devising sufficiently strong incentives to operate over a very short period, but of getting a very sluggish economy to make considerable changes within a reasonable time. In one important respect, therefore, stimulation of economic development differs from economic mobilization. If it is possible to use direct economic incentives within a reasonable time, it is probably desirable to do so, because the ultimate aim is to make the whole economy more responsive to economic pressures.

It is probable that the stimulation of enterprise and the extension of a monetary economy to wider ranges of the population will be promoted by a moderate dose of inflation. Inflation should not go far enough to generate a lack of confidence in the currency, but an increase in prices of 2 or 3 per cent per annum gives a stimulus to enterprise which probably helps to extend the role of enterprise itself. A rate of inflation of 2 or 3 per cent is of course much harder to maintain than price stability, particularly where statistics are poor. The danger of hyperinflation is real, but the need for development is so urgent that this danger must probably be faced.

The government can also exercise an influence on

the economy by influencing relative incomes. In many underdeveloped economies the relative rates of earning in different parts of the government service exercise a strong influence on comparable earnings outside the government machine. By raising the earnings of a particular category of people (e.g., agricultural extension officers), it is possible to enhance their prestige and to insure an increase in the supply, particularly if training is adapted to that end. These techniques are, however, expensive, and may involve very high taxation.

Sometimes, on the contrary, governments attempt to keep down the incomes of particular categories of people below their market value with a view to economizing in the production of a particular service. Many governments have experimented with such techniques in expanding the education service, since it is possible to divert a substantial number of people into the teaching profession by methods other than economic inducements. This tends to make education cheap, but the extent to which the device can be used depends on the effectiveness of alternative pressures to drive people to become teachers. Totalitarian countries of course enjoy an enormous advantage in their command over these alternative pressures, and hence can achieve far more training for a given expenditure. At other times incomes are increased above the market value not so much to increase the supply as to give those who secure employment strong motives of loyalty and discipline. Many countries, for example, pay their police forces considerably more than would be necessary to recruit people of the caliber required, because it is important that posts in the police force should be highly prized so that people will not jeopardize such posts by careless or irregular behavior. This may be relevant to key development posts where discretion and integrity are essential.

The government is thus frequently in a monopolistic position where it can influence incomes of particular groups, and it may be able to promote economic development sometimes by raising and sometimes by lowering the income of particular classes of people, in comparison with what would be earned in an open market.

Governments can often influence the direction of economic development by rationing scarce raw materials or foreign exchange. In the early days of such rationing there is usually a tendency to concentrate exclusively on goods which are unequivocally necessities. Luxury goods are frowned on and necessities encouraged in the allocation of foreign exchange, or fuel, or steel, and it is felt that this enables a country to develop more economically and to avoid the waste of these scarce resources.

It is important, however, if rationing is to be used to promote development, that attention should be given to the concept of rationing key factors with a view to securing predetermined economic consequences, and the rationing should visualize the effects on relative prices, incentives, and relative rates of development in different parts of the economy so as to secure the intended objectives of policy. Various governments have discovered that certain luxury goods serve an important purpose as incentives and that other luxury goods are useful in mopping up purchasing power in the parts of the economy where excess purchasing power is causing trouble.

In peacetime, rationing is not primarily an instrument for securing fair shares or even mitigating inequalities of wealth in a community; but where price movements may be ineffective, rationing can be a powerful instrument. Even in sections of the economy where pricing is effective, results can often be achieved more rapidly and sometimes more economically by rationing than by taxing, particularly if the objective is to economize a given scarce resource.

Perhaps the best known method of influencing the development of an economy is the use of differential taxation. Taxation is more effective in altering relative prices than in directly altering relative incomes. But it can be used very effectively to alter relative incomes, for example, when poll taxes are imposed in order to induce subsistence workers to work for pay. The main difficulty about using taxation primarily as an instrument for influencing relative incomes is that sharp discrimination between different categories of people is usually politically unacceptable, though of course incomes can be influenced indirectly by taxes on particular commodities. A modern undeveloped community will probably not try to break up conservative centers of subsistence agriculture by imposing poll taxes, but it might be willing to levy taxes which would raise the prices of some of the limited number of products which such people bought so as to encourage them to change over to crops which would sell for more money. If, for example, iron or tobacco were made more expensive, workers in a predominately subsistence economy might find that they had to offer more than their previous surplus in exchange in order to maintain their previous standards; and this might generate a series of changes that would convert them into peasants producing crops for a market. It would probably be considered undesirable in a modern state to use such techniques unless they were accompanied by positive measures designed to benefit such a community as it developed toward an exchange economy.

In conclusion, we must draw attention to the cost that economic development inevitably involves. In most underdeveloped economies the cultural pattern is designed to maintain some stability. Usually the population has been fairly stable with a relatively low expectation of life; and frequently the first external impact, which upsets the subsistence economy originally, is the control of certain diseases and the consequent improvement in the expectation of life and rise in the population. This may make other economic developments inevitable, but the changes will certainly interfere with the fabric of custom which may have many cherished values woven into it. As economists we should normally treat these values as basic facts beyond which we should not wish to go, and the fact that the population concerned is compelled to lose some of these values must be regarded as a cost and a hardship whether we, from outside, approve of these values or not.

The economist who is called on in any way to act as an adviser is here faced with a difficult moral problem. There will probably be policies that are physically possible which could promote development rapidly, but which would run counter to the economist's own moral convictions. To take hypothetical examples, an Indian economist might believe that the strength of the Indian administrative machine and the weakness, docility, and conservatism of the Indian peasant combined to make it possible to introduce a strong dictatorship that could transform the Indian economy rapidly by force. Alternatively, a Malayan economist might believe that the significance of foreign trade conducted through the medium of English would make it possible to solve the technical problems of the country by educating its entire population to become English speaking.

The Indian economist might, for religious or political reasons, believe that it would be wrong to use violence to transform his country's economy. The Malayan economist might feel that it would be an affront to national dignity for the whole population to speak a foreign language. The moral problem at issue is whether, as economists, they are entitled to rule such methods out as impossible or whether their role is simply to state the costs involved, persuasively if they can, but doing no more than giving their reasons why they think a solution along these lines would be wrong.

As in many moral problems, we should probably here avoid extreme solutions. If the economist claims the liberty to exclude from consideration any method of economic development of which he disapproves, his advice on development will be little more than a logical exposition of his own political judgments. On the other hand, one must presumably assume that an economist, like any other human being, is entitled to exclude from consideration certain possible actions that do not come within the limits of what is morally tolerable. It would seem doubtful whether the economist would be entitled to rule out as impossible any method of promoting economic development which he suspected would be acceptable to any considerable minority of the population concerned. In such cases the disadvantages might well be presented as costs, with an indication that the economist himself did not consider that the development could be worthwhile at this cost.

People are not in actual fact influenced solely by the desire for improved standards of living in an economic sense. The period of turmoil and disturbance is one which is bound to be painful. Nor can it be certain that the result of the turmoil will be a rise in the standard of living or an improvement of other values which the community would also appreciate. As stated earlier, a rise in population or an exhaustion of land may necessitate economic development even without any expectation of a rise in standards of income. Nevertheless, once the traditional system has been destroyed, it is essential to develop new techniques so that at least there will be a chance of achieving a higher standard of living.

READING LIST

I have taken the opportunity to publish a short classified reading list on the economy of the Federation of Malaya and Singapore, listing with a few exceptions only titles referring to the period since the First World War, and excluding regular departmental reports and annual publications. I have not attempted to cover statistical sources which contain no descriptive material.

A list of the divisions used is given for reference. Normally, each title is listed once only, though a few important sources appear twice.

(A) General
(B) Population Structure
(C) Labor Organization
(D) Land and Land Tenure
(E) Capital
(F) Enterprise and Business Organization
(G) Currency and Banking
(H) National Income
(I) Consumption Patterns and Social Conditions
(J) Administration and Taxation
(K) Transport

(L) Trade
(M) Rubber
(N) Tin
(O) Rice
(P) Other Agriculture and Co-operation
(Q) Fisheries
(R) Industry and Development
(S) Handicrafts and Small Industries

A. General

BAUER, P. T. "Some Aspects of the Malayan Rubber Slump," *Economica*, N. S. XI (November, 1944), 190-198. Some valubale information on trade, revenue, and conditions during this period.

GERMAN, R. L., ED. *Handbook to British Malaya.* London: Malayan Information Agency, 1936. Latest prewar edition of the official general handbook, a compact and useful secondary source.

INTERNATIONAL BANK FOR RECONSTRUCTION AND DEVELOPMENT. *Economic Development of Malaya.* Baltimore: Johns Hopkins Press, 1955. The Report of the Mission to Malaya. Probably the most important single source of material on Malaya's economy. Listed also in other divisions.

LI DUN-JEN. *British Malaya: An Economic Analysis.* New York: The American Press, 1955. Contains a full but not very accurate bibliography. Apparently not based on local knowledge.

LIM TAY BOH, ED. *Problems of the Malayan Economy* ("Background to Malaya Series," No. 10). Singapore: Donald Moore, 1956. A series of radio talks by members of the staff of the University of Malaya on different aspects of the economy for a specially enrolled audience. Background material.

MACKENZIE, K. E. *Economic and Commercial Conditions in the Federation of Malaya and Singapore.* London: H. M. S. O., 1952. The latest available survey for the Department of Overseas Trade. An excellent collection of descriptive and statistical material.

MILLS, LENNOX A. *British Rule in Eastern Asia.* Minneapolis: University of Minnesota Press, 1942. Thorough prewar study of political and economic conditions. Useful references and tables.

NANJUNDAN, S. "Economic Development in Malaya," in Balkrisna Madan, ed., *Economic Problems of Underdeveloped Countries in Asia* (New Delhi: Indian Council of World Affairs [1953]), pp 145-168. A short survey of the new material, presented from an Indian point of view.

PYE, LUCIEN W. *Guerilla Communism in Malaya.* Princeton: Princeton University Press, 1956. Political analysis, useful for interpretation of several economic issues.

SILCOCK, T. H. *The Economy of Malaya* ("Background to Malaya Series," No. 2). Singapore: Donald Moore, 1954. A short essay. No statistical tables.

————. *Dilemma in Malaya.* London: Gollancz, 1949. A short discussion of some postwar political and economic problems.

SINGAPORE, PUBLIC RELATIONS OFFICE (also, MALAYA, DEPARTMENT OF INFORMATION). *Malaya: A Guide for Businessmen and Visitors.* Singapore and Kuala Lumpur: Government Printers, 1955.

SINGTON, DERRICK. *Malaya Perspective* (Fabian Colonial Bureau, "Research Series"). London: Gollancz, 1953. A short political and economic report.

UNITED KINGDOM, COLONIAL OFFICE. *An Economic Survey of the Colonial Empire,* 1937. London: H. M. S. O., 1940.

————. *An Economic Survey of the Colonial Territories. Volume V: The Far Eastern Territories.* London: H. M. S. O., 1955.

UNITED NATIONS ECONOMIC COMMISSION FOR ASIA AND THE FAR EAST. *Annual Economic Survey,* 1953-1956. Chapters on Malaya and British Borneo, though brief, give more analysis of the working of the economy than most other sources, particularly the chapter in the volume for 1953.

B. *Population Structure*

AIYER, K. A. NEELAKANDHA. *Indian Problems in Malaya.* Kuala Lumpur: "The Indian" Office, 1938. Mainly a political essay, but gives some information about the structure of Indian immigration.

CENSUS, 1921, 1931, 1947. See under J. E. NATHAN, C. L. VLIELAND, M. V. DEL TUFO, below.

CHEN TA. *Chinese Migrations, with Special Reference to Labor Conditions* (U. S. Bureau of Labor Statistics, "Bulletin 340"). Washington: Government Printing Office, 1923.

————. *Emigrant Communities of South China.* New York: Institute of Pacific Relations, 1940. Important background information about the sources of Chinese migrants and some economic effects of migration. Appendices on History of Emigration and on Education in the South Seas.

COLE, FAYE-COOPER. *The Peoples of Malaysia.* New York: Van Nostrand, 1945. General description, including Malaya.

DEL TUFO, M. V. *A Report on the 1947 Census of Population.* London: Crown Agents for the Colonies, 1949. Principal source on population structure. Important discussion of prewar immigration pattern.

NATHAN, JULIUS E. *Census of Malaya, 1921.*
London: Waterlow, 1922. Historical emphasis in the
text, with some discussion of early information.

PURCELL, V. W. W. "Chinese Settlement in Malacca," *Journal of the Malayan Branch of the Royal
Asiatic Society,* XX (June, 1947), 115-125. Careful
analysis concerning the earliest permanent settlement of
Chinese in Malaya.

————. *The Chinese in Malaya.* London: Oxford
University Press, 1948. The standard work on this
community, mainly historical in emphasis.

————. *The Chinese in Modern Malaya.* Singapore,
Donald Moore, 1956.

————. *The Chinese in Southeast Asia.* London:
Oxford University Press, 1951.

SILCOCK, T. H. "Migration Problems of the Far
East," in Brinley Thomas, ed., *The Economics of International Migration* (London: Macmillan, 1958), pp.
251-272.

SMITH, T. E. *Population Growth in Malaya.* London: Royal Institute of International Affairs, 1952.
Thorough and detailed study of Malayan demography.

VLIELAND, C. A. *A Report on the 1931 Census.*
London: 1932. Interesting demographic investigations
on relations between migration and natural growth.

WINSTEDT, R. O. *The Malays: A Cultural History.*
London: Paul Kegan, Trench, Trubner & Co., 1947.
This work is probably more useful for an appraisal of the
Malay position in the modern economy than the same
author's *History of Malaya.*

YOU POH SENG. "Fertility and the Increase of
Population in Singapore," *Proceedings of the World
Population Conference* (New York: United Nations,
1955), pp. 989-999. Demographic analysis.

————. "Population of Malaya," in Lim Tay Boh,

ed., *Problems of the Malayan Economy* (Singapore: Donald Moore, 1956), pp. 6-10.

C. Labor Organization

AWBERY, S. S., AND F. W. DALLEY. *Labour and Trade Union Organisation in the Federation of Malaya and Singapore.* Kuala Lumpur: Government Printer, 1948. Survey of the trade union situation just before the outbreak of the emergency.

AZIZ, UNGKU A. "Development and Utilisation of Labour Resources in Southeast Asia," in Philip W. Thayer and W. T. Phillips, *Nationalism and Progress in Free Asia* (Baltimore: Johns Hopkins Press, 1956), pp. 193-203. An analytical paper, mainly on rural labor, read at the Rangoon Conference organized by the Rangoon-Hopkins Center.

BLYTHE, W. L. "History of Chinese Labour in Malaya," *Journal of the Malayan Branch of the Royal Asiatic Society*, XX (June, 1947), 64-114. Important source mainly historical, but giving essential background information.

BROWNE, MAJOR G. ST. J. ORDE. *Report on Labour Conditions in Ceylon, Mauritius and Malaya.* London: H. M. S. O., 1943, Cmd. 6423. References to Malaya are rather brief, but this work is rather more accessible in the U. S. than other sources on labor conditions immediately before the war.

GAMBA, CHARLES. "Data Paper on Labour Organisation and Wage-fixing Tribunals in Malaya." *Proceedings of the Conference of the Pan-Indian Ocean Scientific Association, August, 1954,* Section E. Perth, Western Australia, 1954. Factual summary of the position at the time.

————. *Labour Law in Malaya* ("Background to Malaya Series," No. 8). Singapore: Donald Moore, 1955. A critical paper setting out the positions of labor and trade unionism in Malaya under the law.

————. "Staff Relations in the Government Services of Malaya," *Malayan Economic Review*, II (October, 1957), 12-32. Survey of the development and present position.

————. "Trade Unionism in Malaya," *Far Eastern Survey*, XXIII (February, 1954), 28-30. Comment on the position at the time.

INTERNATIONAL LABOUR ORGANIZATION. *Agricultural Wages and Income of Primary Producers*. Nuwara Eliya, Ceylon: I. L. O. Asian Regional Conference, 1950. Report of the Ceylon Regional Conference.

JOSEY, ALEX. *Trade Unionism in Malaya* ("Background to Malaya Series," No. 4). Singapore: Donald Moore, 1954. Mainly political comment.

LASKER, BRUNO. *Human Bondage in Southeast Asia*. Chapel Hill: University of North Carolina Press, 1950. Explanations of tensions of the time in terms of earlier conditions.

NANJUNDAN, S. *Indians in Malayan Economy*. New Delhi: Office of Economic Adviser, Government of India, 1951.

PILLAI, P. P., ED. *Labour in Southeast Asia*. New Delhi: Indian Council of World Affairs, 1947. General account of the immediate postwar position from an Indian point of view.

SASTRI, SRINIVASA. *Report on the Conditions of Indian Labour in Malaya*. New Delhi: Government of India, 1937. Although the Indian government decided to suspend assisted immigration facilities to Malaya on the basis of this report, the report itself gives a balanced, and not particularly critical, assessment.

SIEW NIM CHEE. *Labour and Tin Mining in Malaya.* Ithaca: Cornell University, Southeast Asia Program, Department of Far Eastern Studies, 1953. Description and analysis based on field work undertaken at the University of Malaya.

THOMPSON, VIRGINIA. *Labor Problems in Southeast Asia.* New Haven: Yale University Press, 1947. A general survey including Malaya. Emphasis mainly political.

D. Land and Land Tenure

(Most titles under Rubber, Other Agriculture and Co-operation, Tin, Administration and Taxation, or General. Some more general titles listed, mainly without comment, below.)

COWGILL, J. V. "The System of Land Tenure in the Federated Malay States," *Malayan Agricultural Journal*, XVI (1928), 181-193.

DOBBY, E. H. G. *Agricultural Questions of Malay.* Cambridge: Cambridge University Press, 1949.

———. "Settlement and Land Utilization, Malacca," *Geographical Journal*, XCIV (December, 1939), 466-478.

———. "Padi Landscapes of Malaya," *Malayan Journal of Tropical Geography*, Vol. VI (October, 1955).

———. "The Kelantan Delta," *Geographical Review*, XLI (April, 1951), 226-255.

———. "Resettlement Transforms Malaya," *Economic Development and Cultural Change*, I (1952) 163-189.

————. "Settlement Patterns in Malaya," *Geographical Review*, XXXII (April, 1942), 211-232.

————. *Southeast Asia*. New York: J. Wiley, 1951.

FEDERATION OF MALAYA. *Committee Appointed by H. E. the High Commissioner to Investigate the Squatter Problem: Report*. Kuala Lumpur: Government Printer, 1949. Origins, characteristics, etc., of illegal settlement, mainly on the jungle fringe.

————, LAND DEVELOPMENT AUTHORITY. *No Need to Be Poor*. Kuala Lumpur: Government Printer, 1957. Policy statement.

JACOBY, E. H. *Agrarian Unrest in Southeast Asia*. New York: Columbia University Press, 1949.

MEEK, C. K. *Land Law and Custom in the Colonies*. 2nd ed. London: Oxford University Press, 1949.

PELZER, K. J. *Pioneer Settlement in the Asiatic Tropics*. New York: American Geographical Society, 1945.

WILSON, T. B. "Some Economic Aspects of Padi Land Ownership in Krian," *Malayan Agricultural Journal*, XXXVII (1954), 125-135.

————. "The Inheritance and Fragmentation of Malay Padi Lands in Krian, Perak," *ibid.*, XXXVIII (1955), 78-91. Important land tenure studies.

E. Capital

CAINE, SIR SIDNEY. "The Importance of Capital," *Malayan Economic Review*, I (August, 1956), 1-5. Brief article emphasizing the importance of capital, particularly local capital, for the development of Malaya.

CALLIS, HELMUT G. *Foreign Capital in Southeast Asia*. New York: Institute of Pacific Relations, 1942.

Survey of the amount of foreign investment, showing entrepreneur capital separately. Some discussion of valuation methods, and also of the significance of different kinds of capital.

CONSULTATIVE COMMITTEE ON ECONOMIC DEVELOPMENT IN SOUTH AND SOUTHEAST ASIA. *The Colombo Plan, Annual Reports.* London: H. M. S. O., 1952-1956. Contain estimates of capital formation and accounts of foreign assistance from various quarters.

GULL, E. M. *British Economic Interests in the Far East.* New York: Institute of Pacific Relations, 1943. General discussion of trade and investment, including that of other Commonwealth countries in the Far East, e.g., Australian interests in Malaya.

MEEK, J. P. *Malaya: A Study of Governmental Response to the Korean Boom.* Ithaca: Cornell University Press, 1955. A study based on analysis of documents and statistics over a limited period. Extensive discussion of alleged capital flight during the period.

REMER, C. F. *Foreign Investments in China.* New York: Macmillan, 1933. Contains information on movements of funds from Malaya to China during the period.

ROYAL INSTITUTE OF INTERNATIONAL AFFAIRS. *The Problem of International Investment.* London: Oxford University Press, 1937. Results of a Chatham House study group investigation. A basis for most subsequent figures about foreign capital in Malaya.

SINGAPORE. *White Paper on the Balance of Payments of Singapore, 1956.* Singapore: Government Printer, 1958, Cmd. 9.

UNITED KINGDOM, COLONIAL OFFICE. *An Economic Survey of the Colonial Empire, 1937.* London:

H. M. S. O., 1940. Industrial establishments classified.

――――. *An Economic Survey of the Colonial Territories. Vol. V: The Far Eastern Territories.* London: H. M. S. O., 1955. Estimates of capital formation.

F. Enterprise and Business Organization

ALLEN, G. C., AND AUDREY G. DONNITHORNE. *Western Enterprise in Indonesia and Malaya.* New York: Macmillan, 1957. A great deal of new information on the operations of the agency houses and banks operating in the area, together with material on all aspects of Western enterprise.

CHEESEMAN, H. R. "The Oldest Malayan Firm— The Story of Guthrie and Co., Ltd.," *Malaya* (January, 1955), pp. 37-40.

――――. "The Second Oldest Malayan Firm, the Story of Boustead and Co.," *Malaya* (January, 1956), pp. 38-40. While these two articles give less information on business organization than the business histories listed below, they give information from the firms' records, bearing on development.

FFORDE, J. S. *An International Trade in Managerial Skills.* Oxford: Blackwell, 1957. Firms operating in Malaya are covered in this stimulating and original analysis.

HARRISONS AND CROSFIELD. *East India Merchant House: 100 Years as India Merchants.* London: Harrisons and Crosfield, 1943.

LONGHURST, H. C. *The Borneo Story.* London: Newman Neame, 1956. These firms' histories together give a good deal of information about past economic development in the area, but they also give information about the structure of business in the trades operated by

Europeans. Information on business structure can also be derived from smaller business histories published by Joseph Travers & Co., Mansfields, the Singapore Cold Storage Co., Ltd., and the following listed elsewhere: The Glen Line, The F. M. S. Railways (Transport); The Chartered Bank (Currency and Credit); and also from Walter Makepeace and Gilbert E. Brooks, eds., *One Hundred Years of Singapore* (London: J. Murray, 1921).

SONG ONG SIANG. *One Hundred Years History of the Chinese in Singapore.* London: J. Murray, 1923. Comments on personalities and families. Of some use as background for the family structure of existing Straits Chinese businesses.

STAHL, KATHLEEN M. *The Metropolitan Organization of British Colonial Trade.* London: Faber & Faber, 1951. Detailed study, mainly arranged by region of operations, of the London controlling institutions.

STRAITS SETTLEMENTS. *Report of a Commission Appointed by H. E. the Governor, to Enquire into and Report on the Trade of the Colony.* 4 vols. Singapore: Government Printer, 1934. Useful source on many aspects of business organization of the period. Now very scarce.

G. Currency and Credit

ANTHONISZ, J. O. *Currency Reform in the Straits Settlements.* London: R. W. Simpson, undated, ca. 1905. Background for the differences between the Malayan currency and other Colonial currency systems.

"Monetary Systems of the Colonies," *The Banker:* "I. Monetary Systems of the Colonies," LXXXVII (July, 1948), 21-24; "IV. Hong Kong," LXXXVIII (October, 1948), 33-39; "V. Malaya" (November,

1948), 101-106; "VIII. Trends and Future Possibilities," LXXXIX (February, 1949), 92-98. This unsigned series gives a concise summary of the position after the Second World War and before independence.

"The Colonies and the Sterling Area," *The Banker*, XCIX (October, 1952), 226-234.

BASTER, A. S. J. *The Imperial Banks*. London: King, 1929.

BAUER, P. T. "Rubber and Foreign Exchange," *Economic Journal*, L (June, 1940), 231-241. Draws attention to a Malayan loop-hole in the original sterling area control system.

BLACKETT, SIR BASIL. *Report on the Malayan Currency*. Kuala Lumpur: Government Printer, 1934. Recommendations which formed the basis of the first joint system, in the 1938 Ordinance.

CLAUSEN, SIR G. "The British Colonial Currency System," *Economic Journal*, LIV (April, 1944), 1-25.

GREAVES, IDA C. *Colonial Monetary Conditions* ("Colonial Research Studies," No. 10). London: H. M. S. O., 1953.

———. "Sterling Balances and the Colonial Currency System: A Comment," *Economic Journal*, LXIII (December, 1953), 921-923.

———. "The Sterling Balances of Colonial Territories," *ibid.*, LXI (June, 1951), 433-439.

HAZLEWOOD, A. D. "The Economics of Colonial Monetary Arrangements," *Social and Economic Studies*, III (December, 1954), 291-315.

———. "Colonial External Finance since the War," *Review of Economic Studies*, XXI, No. 1 (1953-1954), 31-52.

———. "Notes on Sterling Balances and the Colonial Currency System," *Economic Journal*, LXII (December, 1952), 942-945.

————. *Ibid.*, LXIV (September, 1954), 616-617.

KING, F. H. H. "A Note on Sterling Balances and the Colonial Currency System," *Economic Journal*, LXV (December, 1955), 719-721.

————. *Money in British East Asia* ("Colonial Research Studies," No. 19). London: H. M. S. O., 1957.

MACKENZIE, COMPTON. *Realms of Silver.* London: Routledge and Kegan Paul, 1954. Material on the role of one of the leading banks in economic development in the area.

NICULESCU, B. M. "A Note on Sterling Balances and the Colonial Currency System," *Economic Journal*, LXIV (September, 1954), 618-619.

PLUMPTRE, A. W. F. *Central Banking in the British Dominions.* Toronto: Toronto University Press, 1940. Part II gives relevant material on the conditions for establishing central banking, though without reference to Malaya.

PRIDMORE, F. "Coins and Coinages of the Straits Settlements and British Malaya," *Raffles Museum Memoirs*, II. Singapore, 1955.

SHANNON, H. A. "Sterling Balances of the Sterling Area," *Economic Journal*, LX (September, 1950), 531-551.

SHERWOOD, P. W. "The Watson-Caine Report on the Establishment of a Central Bank in Malaya," *Malayan Economic Review*, II (April, 1957), 23-24. A critical discussion of proposed Central Bank powers.

TAN EE LEONG. "The Chinese Banks Incorporated in Singapore and the Federation of Malaya," *Journal of the Malayan Branch of the Royal Asiatic Society*, XXVI

(July, 1953), 113-139. Very useful article illustrating some of the initial difficulties of the establishment of Chinese-owned banks doing business on more or less Western lines.

WATSON, G. M., AND SIR SIDNEY CAINE. *A Central Bank in Malaya, Report on the Establishment of a Central Bank in Malaya.* Kuala Lumpur: Government Printer, 1956. Detailed proposals for constitution and powers. *See also* Technical Report 12 of the International Bank Mission's Report, listed under General.

WILSON, P. A. "Money in Malaya," *Malayan Economic Review,* II (October, 1957), 53-66. A review of the Malayan section of F. H. H. King's book, with statistical material and important new analysis of Malayan monetary arrangements. *See also* Federation of Malaya, Legislative Council Debates, Kuala Lumpur: Government Printer, 1957, cols. 2631-2635, speech by H. S. Lee, Minister of Finance, cited in this article.

H. National Income

AZIZ, U. A. *Economic Survey of Five Villages in Nyalas, Malacca.* Kuala Lumpur: Rural and Industrial Development Authority (mimeographed), 1957. To be issued in printed form shortly by the Government Printer, Kuala Lumpur. Survey material on rural incomes and living conditions. Limited circulation.

BENHAM, F. C. C. *National Income of Malaya, 1947-49.* Singapore: Government Printer, 1951. Important source for the structure of the Malayan economy. New statistical material on entrepôt trade, and several sample enquiries, in addition to original compilation.

————. *Economic Survey of Singapore.* Singapore: Government Printer, 1957. First estimates and breakdown for national income of Singapore separately.

ECKHARDT, H. C., chairman. *Report of the Retrenchment Committee.* Kuala Lumpur: Government Printer, 1932. Part I of this report is believed to be the first attempt to assess Malaya's national income, though it relates only to the old Federated Malay States. The estimates are clearly far too low, as they omit all categories of income locally produced and consumed other than agricultural produce.

GOH KENG SWEE. *Urban Incomes and Housing.* Singapore: Government Printer, 1956. A sample survey of conditions of living, including successful questions on individual and household incomes in Singapore.

INTERNATIONAL BANK FOR RECONSTRUCTION AND DEVELOPMENT. *Economic Development of Malaya.* Baltimore: Johns Hopkins Press, 1955. Contains national income estimates up to 1953.

LIM TAY BOH. "National Income of Malaya, by F. C. C. Benham," *Economica,* XIX (August, 1952), 144-145. Review Article.

SEERS, D. "The Role of National Income Statistics in the Statistical Policy of an Under-developed Country," *Malayan Economic Review,* II (April, 1957), 75-78. A general discussion of this theme with a few special references to Malaya.

SHERWOOD, P. W. "Export Duties and the National Income Accounts," *Economic Journal,* LXVI (March, 1956), 73-83. A general article on this theme, but with special reference to Malaya and other countries in which export duties are important in public finance.

I. Consumption Patterns and Social Conditions

BURGESS, R. O., AND LAIDIN BIN ALANG MUSA. *Report on the State of Health, the Diet and the Economic Conditions of Groups of People in the Lower Income-*

Levels in Malaya ("Institute of Medical Research," Report 13). Kuala Lumpur: Government Printer, September, 1950. Second part contains pioneer work on consumption, possessions, etc.

FIRTH, ROSEMARY. *Housekeeping among Malay Peasants.* (London School of Economics, "Monographs on Social Anthropology," No. 7). London: P. Lund, Humphries & Co., 1946. Very useful source.

GOH KENG SWEE. *Urban Incomes and Housing.* Singapore: Government Printer, 1956.

LIM TAY BOH. "The Planning of Social Security in Malaya," *Malayan Economic Review*, I (August, 1956), 25-36.

MALAYAN UNION AND SINGAPORE. *Joint Wages Commission, Interim Report.* Singapore: Government Printer, 1947. Contains discussion of various trade union and other budgets.

MERRIAM, IDA C. "Social Security and Economic Development," *Malayan Economic Review*, II (October, 1957), 33-42.

ROBERTSON, JEAN. "Social Services and Living Standards," in Lim Tay Boh, *Problems of the Malayan Economy* (Singapore: Donald Moore, 1956), pp. 56-60.

SINGAPORE. *Committee on Minimum Standards of Livelihood Report.* Singapore: Legislative Assembly, 1957, Cmd. 5. Recommendations on minimum wage legislation and on social security.

SINGAPORE. *Report of the Retirement Benefits Commission (F. S. McFadzean, Chairman).* Singapore: Government Printer, 1952.

SINGAPORE ASSOCIATION. *Pensions Provident Fund or Insurance?* Singapore: Straits Times Press, 1955. A discussion of the legislation and of various alternative possibilities.

Singapore, Department of Social Welfare. *Social Survey of Singapore.* Singapore: Government Printer, 1947. Information on family living patterns, housing, education, etc.

Singapore, Department of Statistics. *Malaya.* Singapore: Government Printer, 1948. The 1948 issue of this annual publication contains as an appendix the results of the Pilot Survey for a budget survey which was never carried out. The range is too limited, but until the survey now being conducted is published it is the only material of its kind available.

Vickers, W. J., and J. H. Strahan. *Health Survey of the State of Kedah.* Kuala Lumpur: Kyle Palmer and Co., 1935-1936. Limited material on nutrition.

You Poh Seng. "The Housing Survey of Singapore, 1955," *Malayan Economic Review*, II (April, 1957), 54-74. Survey undertaken by a University of Malaya team of social workers in training.

J. Administration and Taxation

Benham, F. C. C. *Report on the Trade of Penang.* Kuala Lumpur: Government Printer, 1948. Discusses the free port issue.

Carnell, F. G. "British Policy in Malaya," *Political Quarterly*, XXIII (July, 1952), 269-281.

————. "Constitutional Reform and Elections in Malaya," *Pacific Affairs*, XXVII (September, 1954), 216-235.

Chin Kee Onn. *Malaya Upside Down.* Singapore: Jitts, 1946. This book gives some estimates of economic conditions during the Japanese occupation, among much other material.

Corry, W. C. S. *A General Survey of New Vil-*

lages. Kuala Lumpur: Government Printer, 1954. Official study of some of the results of the resettlement of rural populations.

EMERSON, R. *Malaysia, A Study in Direct and Indirect Rule.* New York: Macmillan, 1937. Thorough prewar study. Emphasis mainly political.

FEDERATION OF MALAYA. *The Federation of Malaya Agreement, 1948.* Kuala Lumpur: Government Printer, 1952.

————. *Federation of Malaya Agreement (Amendment).* Ordinance 39, of 1955.

————. *Report of the Committee on Financial Provisions of the Federation of the Malaya Agreement, 1948.* Kuala Lumpur: Government Printer, 1955. Council Paper 29/55.

————. *Report of the Penang Customs Duties Working Party.* Kuala Lumpur: Government Printer, 1956. Council Paper 51.

HUAN TZU HONG. "The New System of Revenue Allocation to the States and Settlements in the Federation of Malaya," *Malayan Economic Review,* II (April, 1957), 79-83.

JONES, S. W. *Public Administration in Malaya.* New York and London: Royal Institute of International Affairs, 1953. Historical account of developments in government in recent times from an administrator's point of view.

KING, F. H. H. *The New Malayan Nation, A Study of Communalism and Nationalism.* New York: Institute of Pacific Relations, 1957. Brief factual and interpretative study, mainly of the Reid Constitutional Proposals.

LIM TAY BOH. "Income Redistribution in Underdeveloped Territories," in A. T. Peacock, ed., *Income Redistribution and Social Policy; a set of studies* (London; Jonathan Cape, 1954), pp. 268-290.

MARKANDAN, P. *The Problems of the New Villages in Malaya.* Singapore: Donald Moore, 1955.

MILLS, L. A., AND ASSOCIATES. *The New World of Southeast Asia.* Minneapolis: University of Minnesota Press, 1949.

ONN BIN JAFFAR, DATO SIR. *Report on Community Development in the Federation of Malaya.* Kuala Lumpur: Government Printer, 1954. Report and recommendations of a Conference at Taiping.

PEET, G. L. *Political Questions of Malaya.* Cambridge: Cambridge University Press, 1949. Background essay on the political problems of the time.

PURCELL, V. W. W. *Malaya, Outline of a Colony.* London: Nelson, 1946.

————. *Malaya, Communist or Free?* London: Gollancz, 1954. The first of these gives a brief outline of the immediate postwar position; the second, a vigorous attack on the policies of General Templer. Dr. Purcell's more important work is listed under Population Structure.

UNITED KINGDOM. *Constitutional Proposals for the Federation of Malaya.* London: H. M. S. O., 1957, Cmd. 210.

K. Transport

ALLEN, D. F. *Reports on the Major Ports of Malaya.* Kuala Lumpur: Government Printer, 1951.

————. *Report on the Minor Ports of Malaya.* Kuala Lumpur: Government Printer, 1952. Two official reports giving advice on general port development, including the development of Port Swettenham.

FEDERATED MALAY STATES RAILWAYS. *Fifty Years of Railways in Malaya, 1885-1935.* Kuala Lumpur: F. M. S. Railway, 1935. Memoir giving convenient summary of development, operating revenue, etc.

FEDERATION OF MALAYA, FEDERAL PORTS COMMITTEE. *Report and Supplementary Report.* Kuala

Lumpur: Government Printer, 1952.   Official consideration of the two by Allen, above.

GLEN LINE.   *Achievements of the Glen and Shire
Shipping Lines, 1869-1949.*   London: Glen Line, 1949.

SANDERS, J. O.   "The Malayan Railways," *Malaya*
(September, 1952), 25-28.   Useful source by a former
general manager of the Malayan Railways, especially on
post-war recovery and emergency conditions.

UNITED KINGDOM, COLONIAL OFFICE.   *An Economic Survey of the Colonial Empire, 1937.*   London:
H. M. S. O., 1940.

————.   *An Economic Survey of the Colonial Territories.   Volume V: The Far Eastern Territories.*   London: H. M. S. O., 1955.   One of the few sources, other
than annual reports, on road development.

L. Trade

CAINE, SIR S.   "Instability of Primary Product
Prices: A Protest and a Proposal," *Economic Journal,*
LXIV (September, 1954), 610-614.   Raises some im-
portant questions on the effect of instability of prices on
Malayan development.

LEUBUSCHER, CHARLOTTE.   *Processing of Colonial
Raw Materials.*   London: H. M. S. O., 1951.

MAKEPEACE, W., AND GILBERT E. BROOKE, EDS.
One Hundred Years of Singapore.   London: J. Murray,
1921.   Some description of the organization of trade
at the time.

MAXWELL, SIR G.   "The Malay in Commerce,"
United Empire, XXXIX (January-February, 1948),
36-39.   Some ideas on Malay development which have
since gained wider currency.

MEYER, F. V.   *Britain's Colonies in World Trade.*
London: Oxford University Press, 1948.   Regional

treatment, giving a good deal of information about Malaya's trade pattern.

SILCOCK, T. H., chairman. *Singapore Hawkers Inquiry Commission Report.* Singapore: Government Printer, 1950. Contains a survey of street hawkers in Singapore undertaken for the Commission, as well as discussions of street trading conditions.

SOVANI, N. V. *Economic Relations of India with Southeast Asia and the Far East.* Bombay: Oxford University Press, 1949. Statistics and analysis of trade and migration, including Malaya.

STRAITS SETTLEMENTS. *Commission Appointed by H. E. the Governor of the Straits Settlements to Enquire into and Report on the Trade of the Colony, Report.* Singapore: Government Printer, 1934. A full commission of enquiry of which a large part of the evidence was published giving a great deal of information about the trade and shipping conditions at the time.

WILSON, JOAN. *The Singapore Rubber Market.* Singapore: Donald Moore, 1958. Brief description of the working of the market.

M. Rubber

BAUER, P. T. *The Rubber Industry: A Study in Competition and Monopoly.* Cambridge: Harvard University Press, 1948. Standard work on this industry.

————. *Report on a Visit to Rubber Growing Smallholdings in Malaya,* July-September, 1946 ("Colonial Research Publication," No. 1). London: H. M. S. O., 1948. A rather controversial report on a great deal of important research into the smallholding side of the industry. Evidence on smallholding yields.

————. "Rubber Production Costs during the Great Depression," *Economic Journal,* LIII (December, 1943), 861-869.

————. "The Working of Rubber Regulation," *ibid.*, LIV (September, 1946), 391-414. Contains discussion of underassessment of smallholders. *Cf.* Benham and Silcock, below.

————. "The Working of Rubber Regulation: A Rejoinder," *ibid.*, LVIII (June, 1948), 236-243.

————. "Notes on Cost," *Economica*, N. S. XII (May, 1945), 90-100. Article mainly on costs in Malayan rubber industry.

————. "Economics of Planting Density in Rubber Growing," *ibid.*, XIII (May, 1946), 131-135. Very important article.

————. "Malayan Rubber Policies," *ibid.*, XIV (May, 1947), 81-107.

————. "Malayan Rubber Policies," *India Rubber World*, CXVI (August-September, 1947), 629-634; 783-786. Criticism of postwar planting policy.

————. "Malayan Rubber Policy," *Political Science Quarterly*, LXXII (March, 1957), 83-99. More recent criticism on similar lines.

BENHAM, F. C. C. "The Rubber Industry," *Economica*, XVI (November, 1949), 355-368. Review article.

COOK, J. "Purchase and Bulk Processing of Smallholding Latex," *Malayan Agricultural Journal*, XXXIII (July, 1950), 136-143.

————. "Further Notes on the Marketing of Smallholding Latex," *ibid.*, XXXVI (July, 1953), 181-189.

FEDERATION OF MALAYA. *Taxation and Replanting in the Rubber Industry*. Kuala Lumpur: Government Printer, 1955. Statement of government policy and analysis of Mudie Report and proposals of Rubber Producers' Council—summarized in appendix.

FIGART, D. M. *The Plantation Rubber Industry in*

the Middle East. Washington: Government Printing Office, 1925. Material on capital formation and other aspects of the industry in its early years.

GAMBA, C. *Synthetic Rubber and Malaya.* ("Background to Malaya Series," No. 11). Singapore: Donald Moore, 1956. Analysis of the synthetic rubber threat.

GRIST, D. H. *Nationality of Ownership and Nature of Constitution of Rubber Estates in Malaya.* ("Straits Settlements Agricultural Department Bulletin, Economic Series," No. 2). Kuala Lumpur: Government Printer, 1933.

KELLETT, W. W. "International Rubber Statistics," *Journal of the Royal Statistical Society,* CXII, Pt. 4 (1949), 419-435. A full and critical survey of statistical material.

KNORR, K. E. *World Rubber and Its Regulation.* Stanford: Stanford University Press, 1945. Standard commodity control study.

McFADYEAN, SIR A., ED. *History of Rubber Regulation, 1934-43.* London: Norton, 1944. Account of regulation from the plantation industry's point of view.

MEADS, H. D. *Bark Consumption and Bark Reserves on Rubber Smallholdings in Malaya.* ("Straits Settlement Agricultural Department Bulletin, Economic Series," No. 4). Kuala Lumpur: Government Printer, 1934. Early study of a subject which later became an issue of economic discussion.

MUDIE, SIR F., chairman. *Report of the Mission of Inquiry into the Rubber Industry of Malaya.* Kuala Lumpur: Government Printer, 1954. Commission suggesting rather more far-reaching measures to aid the industry than those actually implemented.

RAE, G. "Statistics of the Rubber Industry," *Journal of the Royal Statistical Society,* CI (1938), 317 ff.

Fairly full prewar survey but needs to be supplemented by Bauer's work on this period.

Rowe, J. W. F. "Rubber," in *Studies in the Artificial Control of Raw Material Supplies,* London: Royal Economic Society, 1930.

————. "Rubber," in *Markets and Men,* New York: Macmillan, 1936. Excellent early studies of this period of the Regulation scheme in economic terms.

Silcock, T. H. "A Note on the Working of Rubber Regulation," *Economic Journal,* LVIII (June, 1948), 228-235. Critical comment on some of Bauer's estimates and interpretations.

Soliva, R. J. H. *An Economic View of Rubber Planting.* Singapore: Kelly and Walsh, 1931. Early cost and return analysis of rubber planting from a business point of view.

Whitford, H. N. *Estate and Native Plantation Rubber in the Middle East.* New York: Rubber Manufacturers Association of America, 1930. See also four other reports on Natural Rubber for the Rubber Manufacturers Association, 1928-1935, by the same author, cited by P. T. Bauer in *The Rubber Industry.*

Whittlesey, C. R. *Governmental Control of Crude Rubber: The Stevenson Plan.* Princeton: Princeton University Press, 1931. Study of rubber regulation mainly from consumers' point of view.

N. Tin

Eastham, J. K. "Rationalisation in the Tin Industry," *Review of Economic Studies,* IV (October, 1936), 13-32. Very important but neglected early study of tendencies to monopoly in tin and also of importance of asset values.

Elliott, W. Y., and Others. *International Con-*

trol in the Non-ferrous Metals. New York: Macmillan, 1937. Factual study of tin and other control schemes. Information about techniques from economists' point of view.

FERGUSON, SIR E. "Singapore and Tin," *Malaya* (March, 1955) pp. 39, 49. Popular treatment giving postwar facts about smelting, etc., by leader of the industry.

FERMOR, SIR L. *Report upon the Mining Industry of Malaya.* Kuala Lumpur: Government Printer, 1940. Full and thorough analysis based on an official enquiry into the industry.

JONES, W. R. *Tinfields of the World.* London: Mining Publishers Ltd., 1925. General survey, including Malaya, which first caused serious concern about world's future reserves of tin.

KNORR, K. E. *Tin Under Control.* Stanford: Stanford University Press, 1945. Standard commodity control study.

ROWE, J. W. F. "Tin," in *Markets and Men* (New York: Macmillan, 1936), pp. 152-168.

SIEW NIM CHEE. "The International Tin Agreement, 1953," *Malayan Economic Review,* II (April, 1957), 35-53. Factual survey and assessment mainly from standpoint of equity and viability.

U. N. TIN CONFERENCE. *1953 International Tin Agreement.* Kuala Lumpur: Government Printer, 1953.

U. S. CONGRESS, SENATE SUBCOMMITTEE OF THE COMMITTEE ON THE ARMED SERVICES. *Sixth Report on Preparedness.* Washington: Government Printing Office, 1951.

————, PREPAREDNESS SUBCOMMITTEE OF THE COMMITTEE ON THE ARMED SERVICES. *Stockpiling of Tin and Rubber, Hearings.* Washington: Government

Printing Office, 1951. Critical survey of monopolistic tendencies and other features of control over output of tin.

O. Rice

ALLEN, E. F., AND D. W. M. HAYNES. "A Review of Investigations into the Mechanical Cultivation and Harvesting of Wet Padi with special reference to the latter," *Malayan Agricultural Journal,* XXXVI April, 1953), 61-80.

DOBBY, E. H. G. "Malaya's Rice Problem," *Pacific Affairs,* XXVII (March, 1954), 58-60.

FEDERATED MALAY STATES. *Rice Cultivation Committee Report.* Kuala Lumpur: Government Printer, 1931.

―――. DEPARTMENT OF AGRICULTURE. *Report on the Progress of Schemes for the Extension of Rice Cultivation.* Kuala Lumpur: Government Printer, 1935.

FEDERATION OF MALAYA. *Report of the Rice Production Committee.* Kuala Lumpur: Government Printer, 1953.

―――. *Rice Committee Interim Report.* Kuala Lumpur: Government Printer, 1955.

―――. *Rice Committee Final Report.* Kuala Lumpur: Government Printer, 1956. The first two reports show the nature of prewar official emphasis on rice production, and the efforts made to deter movement away from rice as well as to extend acreage. The third surveys a good deal of detail but appears to underestimate economic factors. The fourth is a brief set of recommendations for dealing with a fall in rice prices. The fifth is a full survey with considerable economic analysis.

GRIST, D. H. "Rice in Malaya in 1940," *Malayan Agricultural Journal*, XXIX (April, 1941), 155-162. Last of a series of annual prewar summaries. Review of prewar developments and wartime conditions.

HAYNES, D. W. M. "Calculation of Costs of Mechanical Operations with Particular Reference to the Mechanical Harvesting of Rice," *Malayan Agricultural Journal*, XXXVII (January, 1954), 54-67.

————. "Preliminary Survey of Transport Methods in Padi Areas, with Special Reference to Problems of Mechanical Harvesting," *Malayan Agricultural Journal*, XXXVII (July, 1954), 146-153.

————. "The Use of Self Propelled Combine Harvesters for the Harvesting of Wet Padi in the North Kedah Plain," *Malayan Agricultural Journal*, XXXVII (July, 1954), 68-90.

————. "Further Investigations into the Use of Self-Propelled Combine Harvesters for Wet Padi in North Kedah," *Malayan Agricultural Journal*, XXXVIII (October, 1955), 237-249.

HILL, A. T. "Kelantan Padi Planting," *Journal of the Malayan Branch of the Royal Asiatic Society*, XXIV (February, 1951), 55-76. Mainly a study of techniques from an anthropological point of view.

THOMSON, A. M. *Report on the Marketing of Rice in the Federation of Malaya* ("Food and Agricultural Organization Report," No. 278). New York: United Nations, 1954.

WICKIZER, V. D., AND M. K. BENNETT. *Rice Economy of Monsoon Asia*. Stanford: Stanford University Press, 1957. General survey showing Malaya in the South Asian context. Emphasis not economic.

P. Other Agriculture and Co-operation

AZIZ, U. A. "Some Aspects of the Malayan Rural Economy Related to Measures of Mobilizing Savings," UNECAFE, *Report and Documents of First Working Party on Mobilization of Domestic Capital* (Bangkok: 1952), pp. 188-193.

————. "Facts and Fallacies of Malay Economy," four articles in *Straits Times*, Singapore, February 28 to March 5, 1957, reissued as Convention paper by Malayan Students Merdeka Convention. London: Malaya Hall, 1957.

BARNETT, H. L. "A Brief Review of Essential Foodcrop Cultivation in Malaya," *Malayan Agricultural Journal*, XXX (January, 1947), 13-19. Outline of immediate postwar position with indications of impact of war shortages on cultivation.

BURKILL, I. H. *Dictionary of the Economic Products of the Malay Peninsula*. London: Crown Agents, 1935. Reference material on many crops and products giving uses and information about customs.

CHEESEMAN, E. E. *Cultivation of Cocoa*. London: H. M. S. O., 1948. Report on an official investigation; the basis of recent cocoa developments.

COURTENAY, C. E. "Reconstruction of the Malayan Canned Pineapple Industry," *Malayan Agricultural Journal*, XXX (October, 1947), 183-190. Account of prewar industry and survey of postwar problems.

————. "Malayan Pineapples," three articles in *Malaya* (July, August, September, 1952), 30-32. Popular treatment but much information about postwar developments not elsewhere available.

FABIAN COLONIAL BUREAU. *Cooperation in the Colonies*. London: Allen and Unwin, 1945. Relatively limited discussion of Malaya.

FIRTH, R. W. "The Peasants of Southeast Asia," *International Affairs,* XXVI (October, 1950), 503-514.

FOOD AND AGRICULTURAL ORGANIZATION. *Problems of Food and Agricultural Expansion in the Far East.* Rome, 1955.

GRIST, D. H. *Outline of Malayan Agriculture.* ("Malayan Planting Manual," No. 2). Kuala Lumpur: Department of Agriculture, 1933, repr. 1950. The standard work on Malayan agricultural practice. Essential material on many agricultural problems.

HAYNES, D. W. M. "A Census of Agricultural Machinery in the Federation of Malaya, 1956," *Malayan Agricultural Journal,* XXXIX (July, 1956), 200-216. Only large estates and Government. Census of smallholders unsuccessful.

KENNAWAY, M. J. *Some Agricultural Enterprises in Malaya, 1933-4.* London: Kennaway Neame and Co., 1934. Reprints from *Straits Times,* etc. An interesting, non-technical sketch of certain individual Malayan agricultural enterprises at the time of the great depression.

LE MARE, D. W. "Pig Rearing, Fish-Farming and Vegetable Growing," *Malayan Agricultural Journal,* XXXV (July, 1952), 156-166. Brief account of Chinese mixed farming in Malaya, and a large-scale experiment with similar techniques.

LIM TAY BOH. *The Cooperative Movement in Malaya.* Cambridge: Cambridge University Press, 1950. Short descriptive account with some analysis.

PIM, SIR A. *Colonial Agricultural Production.* London: Oxford University Press, 1946.

SIMPSON, H. J., AND LAU SING NAM. "Chinese

Market Gardening," *Malayan Agricultural Journal,* XXII (March, 1933), 119-124.

SMITH, A. C. "Coconut Industry in Malaya," *Malaya* (December, 1952), pp. 26-27.

STRICKLAND, C. F. *Cooperation in Malaya.* Kuala Lumpur: Government Printer, 1929. An account of the early development of the movement.

VOELCKER, O. J. "Cocoa from Malaya" *Malaya,* (July, 1955), pp. 49-50.

WICKIZER, V. D. *Coffee, Tea and Cocoa: An Economic and Political Analysis.* Stanford: Stanford University Press, 1957. Not primarily concerned with Malaya but covers some relevant Malayan developments.

Q. Fisheries

BURDON, T. W. *Fishing Industry of Singapore* ("Background to Malaya Series," No. 5). Singapore: Donald Moore, 1955. An essay containing much economic as well as technical information.

————. "Fishing Methods of Singapore," *Journal of the Malayan Branch of the Royal Asiatic Society,* XXVII (June, 1954), 5-76. Description of gear, methods, and location, but no economic analysis.

FEDERATION OF MALAYA GOVERNMENT, COMMITTEE TO INVESTIGATE THE FISHING INDUSTRY. *Report.* Kuala Lumpur: Government Printer, 1956. (Council Paper No. 39.)

FIRTH, R. W. *Malay Fishermen: Their Peasant Economy.* London: Kegan Paul, 1956. Anthropological survey with strong economic emphasis.

————. "Economics of a Malayan Fishing Industry," *Man,* XLI (July-August, 1941), 69-73.

GOPINATH, K. "The Malayan Purse Seine (pukat

jerut) Fishery," *Journal of the Malayan Branch of the Royal Asiatic Society*, XXIII (August, 1950), 75-96. Gives some limited economic analysis of the method of operation.

KESTEVEN, G. L. *Malayan Fisheries Handbook*. Singapore: Malaya Publishing House, 1949.

LE MARE, D. W. "Malaya's Fishing Industry," *Malaya* (July, 1954), 390-393. Popular discussion of development in fisheries by the Director of Fisheries for Malaya and Singapore.

PARRY, M. L. "The Fishing Methods of Kelantan and Trengganu," *Journal of the Malayan Branch of the Royal Asiatic Society*, XXVII (June, 1954), 77-144. Description of gear and operation in postwar methods.

R. *Industry and Development*

BENHAM, F. C. C. *The Colombo Plan and Other Essays*. London: Royal Institute of International Affairs, 1956.

BUTLER, HAROLD. *Problems of Industry in the East with Special Reference to India, French India, Ceylon, Malaya, and the Netherlands Indies.* ("International Labor Office, Studies and Reports," B-29). Geneva: International Labor Office, 1938.

CONSULTATIVE COMMITTEE ON ECONOMIC DEVELOPMENT IN SOUTH AND SOUTHEAST ASIA (COLOMBO PLAN). *Annual Reports*, 1952, 1954, 1955, 1956, 1957. London: H. M. S. O. Valuable information about the progress of development in comparison with other areas.

FEDERATION OF MALAYA. *Draft Development Plan*. Kuala Lumpur: Government Printer, 1950. The first development plan not implemented in this form on account of the Emergency.

―――. *Report of the Industrial Development Working Party.* Kuala Lumpur: Government Printer, 1957. Outline of government policy on industrialization.

―――. *Progress Report on the Development Plan.* Kuala Lumpur: Government Printer, 1953. Some discussion of modification in the plan.

―――. *Report on Economic Planning in the Federation of Malaya.* Kuala Lumpur: Government Printer, 1957. Financial outline of intentions and development.

FIENNES, E. M. *Report on Rural and Industrial Development Authority 1950-55.* Kuala Lumpur: Government Printer, 1956. A critical survey of the work of the authority which led to considerable changes in policy.

FIRTH, R. W. "Money, Work and Social Change in Indo-Pacific Economic Systems," *International Social Science Bulletin,* VI, No. 3 (1954), 400-410. An interesting paper on the frontiers between anthropology and economics with some Malayan material.

GAMBA, C., AND U. A. AZIZ. "RIDA and Malayan Economic Development," *Far Eastern Survey,* XX (October 10, 1951), 173-176.

HAYNES, A. S. "Industrialisation as an Indispensable Means of Maintaining the Level of Prosperity in Tropical Regions: the Position of Malaya," *Comptes Rendus du Congrès International de Géographie,* Tome 11 (Leyden: Brill, 1938), Section IIIc, pp. 543-549.

INTERNATIONAL BANK FOR RECONSTRUCTION AND DEVELOPMENT. *Economic Development of Malaya.* Baltimore: Johns Hopkins Press, 1955. Comprehensive review of Malayan development problems.

Lim Tay Boh. "The Theory and Reality of Economic Development," in P. W. Thayer and W. T. Phillips, *Nationalism and Progress in Free Asia* (Baltimore: Johns Hopkins Press, 1956), pp. 179-192.

Rao, V. K. R. V. "The Colombo Plan for Economic Development," *Lloyds Bank Review*, No. 21 (July, 1951), 12-32.

Shell Co. Ltd. "Shell in Singapore and Borneo," *Malaya* (August, 1955), pp. 29-32.

Shepherd, Jack. *Industry in Southeast Asia.* New York: Institute of Pacific Relations, 1941.

Silcock, T. H. "Some Problems of Economic Growth in the British Territories in Southeast Asia," *Weltwirtschaftliches Archiv*, Band 80, Heft 2 (Hamburg, 1958).

————. "Some Determinants of Economic Development," *Malayan Economic Review*, II (April, 1957), 1-15. Both these articles touch on Malayan problems among others.

S. Handicrafts and Small Industries

Hill, A. H. "The Weaving Industry in Trengganu," *Journal of the Malayan Branch of the Royal Asiatic Society*, XXII (August, 1949), 76-84.

————. "Kelantan Silver Work," *Journal of the Malayan Branch of the Royal Asiatic Society*, XXIV (February, 1951), 99-108.

Morgan, G. T. M. deM. "Brass and White Metal Work in Trengganu," *Journal of the Malayan Branch of the Royal Asiatic Society*, XXIV (October, 1951), 114-119.

Wilkinson, R. J., ed. *Papers on Malay Subjects* ("Malayan Industries"). Kuala Lumpur: Government Printer, 1907-1915: R. Winstedt, "Arts and Crafts," 1909; R. Winstedt, "Fishing, Hunting and Trapping," 1911; G. E. Shaw, "Rice Planting," 1911. All studies primarily from an anthropological point of view. Background only.

INDEX

Agency houses, role of, 102-104, 118, 119

Agriculture: and forest conservation, 36-37; in Malaya, 15-18, 62; prospects for, 115-117, 165-166, 171-172; research in, 113-114; and transportation, 112-113. *See also* Land development

Allen, G. C., 118 n.

Anthonisz, J. O., 120 n.

Areca nuts, 39

Atjeh, 40

Atlantic Charter, 90

Atomic bomb, 61

Australia, 7, 93, 144, 148, 172

Austria, 160

Autonomy. *See* Self-government *and* Political patterns

Aziz, Ungku A., 16 n., 61 n., 158 n.

Balfour, Marshall C., 5 n.

Bali, 164

Banking. *See* Central Bank

Bauer, P. T., 9 n., 11 n., 12 n., 13 n., 84 n., 85 n., 112 n., 113 n., 114 n., 178 n.

Bay of Bengal, 57

Belgium, 159, 164

Belshaw, C. S., 178 n.

Benham, F. C. C., 39 n., 42, 43 n., 48 n., 115 n., 117 n., 157 n.

Birth control, 133

Boeke, J. H., 72 n.

British Borneo Timber Company, 35

Brooke family, 19, 30, 72, 82

Brunei, 7, 37, 44; development after World War II, 72-77;